"John Dear has walked [down the] mountain of instruction [...] into the garden of angu[ish ...] nuclear weaponry and h[as ...] unspeakable jails. He has trekked about the world bearing the gospel in hand and heart, a wing-shod messenger of peace. He has lived in solidarity with the wretched of the earth–whose plight, as he well knows, is the mean feat of abominable economics and killer instincts on rampage. In this century, in this land, cleft in fragments of gigantic disorder, what a witness!"

Daniel Berrigan: priest, anti–war activist;
author, *The Trouble With Our State*

"John Dear has been arrested in the cause of peace and human decency more times than anyone else I know. I am honored to consider him a friend."

Joan Baez: musician and activist

"Some teachers are all theory and some are all practice. John Dear has earned ability to be both. Some teachers are very orthodox and some open new ground. John Dear puts the two together knowing they are the same."

Richard Rohr: Franciscan friar, ecumenical teacher; author,
Falling Upward, The Universal Christ

THE SACRAMENT OF CIVIL DISOBEDIENCE

JOHN DEAR

Foreword by Shane Claiborne

2022 Revised Edition Edited by
Christopher Donald and Sue Parfitt

Published by LAB / ORA Press
A working name for the Congregation of the Passion

St. Peter's Community Centre
Charles Street
Coventry
CV1 5NP
United Kingdom

Second edition published 2022
Edited by Christopher Donald and Sue Parfitt

First published in the UK in 1994 by Fortkamp

Cover design by Benji Spence

ISBN: 978-1-7397162-2-6
Ebook ISBN: 978-1-7397162-3-3

Printed and bound in the United Kingdom by IngramSpark

For Jim and Shelley Douglass,
Friends and Peacemakers

A Note from the Editors ... ix

Foreword ... xiii

Introduction ... 3

PART ONE

Our Tradition of Disobedience

ONE **A Different Way is Possible** ... 15

TWO **We Will Not Serve Your False God** ... 35

THREE **The Revolution of Nonviolence is at Hand** ... 61

FOUR **We Must Obey God Rather than People** ... 97

FIVE **Blessing the Empire** ... 123

CONTENTS

INTERLUDE **A New History** ... 149

PART TWO

Civil Disobedience Field Guide

SIX **There Comes a Time to Cross the Line** ... 165

SEVEN **Preparing to Act** ... 183

EIGHT **Anything Can Happen** ... 215

NINE **Testifying to the Truth** ... 229

TEN **Imprisoned for Sacramental Peacemaking** ... 253

Epilogue ... 293
References ... 299

A Note from the Editors

Towards the end of 2019, I (Sue) spent 3 months in Hebron with the Human Rights organisation, Christian Peacemaker Teams. It was not long before I discovered a small room in the house which doubled as a library and within this little library, a book entitled *The Sacrament of Civil Disobedience*. I found the title engaging—provocative—so I took the book away to glance at, as I thought, when a moment of free time presented itself. This was usually in bed at night, feeling only moderately safe, as my room was overlooked by the glaring lights of our next door neighbours, the Israeli Army, located in the military watchtower. We were often disturbed by the sound of gunfire.

I was soon riveted by this unusual book, and I can honestly say that it had such a profound effect on me that it turned out to be a game-changer in terms of my spiritual life, giving me a new way of understanding my latter years and their possible purpose, bringing me to see them in an entirely new light.

The Sacrament of Civil Disobedience was written in the 1990's by a young Roman Catholic Priest, John Dear, who was at that time a Jesuit. The book describes the roots of nonviolent civil disobedience from the perspective of a Christian, called to follow Jesus in daily discipleship, walking in His footsteps on the way of the Cross.

It explores the Biblical roots of nonviolent civil disobedience, and the way in which the experience of the Early Church was that of frequent arrest, conviction, trial and imprisonment—which, for several hundred years, those who espoused the Christian faith viewed as the normal pattern of life.

In recent years it has been the peace movement which has provided the crucible for many Christians and others, both in Europe and the US, to learn about civil disobedience and to apply some of the learning that had taken place during the abolition of slavery in the US and Britain; the Civil rights movement in America; the struggle for independence in India; the suffragette movement in the US and Europe; and more recently, the anti-apartheid struggle in South Africa. All were characterised by the ambition to remain nonviolent, even if this was not always entirely possible in practice. Likewise, the peace movement, by its very nature, was and is characterised by nonviolence because of the internal logic of the cause that it espouses.

Unfortunately, this wonderful book by John Dear, which has so much to teach the Church as it faces the new challenge of the climate catastrophe, was out of print. I entered into discussion with John about the possibility of getting it updated and re-printed to reflect the needs of the current climate crisis, which has overtaken in its urgency even the terrible threat of nuclear war.

Christians are hearing the call anew to step up to the plate and confront governments with the radical action that is required, if we are not to condemn practically all life on earth to extinction. But we need to step back and discern what exactly God is calling us to do and we need materials to aid our study and prayer. We need John's book but in a new form, updated and directed now to the changed circumstances in which we live, and focussed toward the churches in the UK and Europe as well as towards those in America.

Although John felt unable to lay aside his many other commitments and redesign the original book, another fortuitous connection arrived. The Passionists in England and Wales—another Catholic order—are committed members of the climate movement, embracing protest, ignomy and imprisonment as acts of solidarity with the suffering planet. Working with the Passionists, I (Chris) had started Lab/ora Press, a new publishing imprint, working on re-publishing theological books that were no longer available.

John put us in touch with each other and gave us the freedom to revise and update his original text. So this book is a re-presentation of John's original work, edited and refocussed towards civil disobedience in an age of impending climate catastrophe. It is an attempt to plug the gap in the literature of civil resistance and to provide a road map for Christians contemplating "crossing the line" into civil disobedience now.

As editors of this new edition, we owe the greatest debt of gratitude to John for allowing us to revise and update his text in the way we have. We hope that none of the core teaching of John's original book has been lost but that something has been gained in relevance and applicability by adapting the text and, in some places, refocusing its riches towards the climate crisis. We hope that John's teaching, now re-published at last, may serve to help re-awaken the prophetic voice of the Churches so that they step forward and help lead the way in confronting the forces of evil that have led the creatures on planet earth to the brink of destruction. May it help, even at this late hour, to protect the beautiful creation that God has made.

— *Christopher Donald and Sue Parfitt*
Editors of the 2022 Edition

Foreword

Shane Claiborne

I was speaking at an event in New Mexico, where John lived for many years. He came by and whisked me from the event to visit his magical desert monastery of sorts. On the windy dirt road to his cabin, we saw prairie dogs, road runners, tumbleweed and wild cacti; we even saw a tarantula or two. That was all fantastic, but nothing quite prepared me for what was next. John's house—that's what I remember most. It was like a museum for the movement. His walls were adorned with little personally-written notes, from Joan Baez, Fred Rogers, Mother Teresa.

It was magical. I'd only seen one other place quite like it, and it belonged to John's partner in crime: Fr. Dan Berrigan's house was similarly decorated with newspaper clippings, photos and little relics and gifts. And of course, Dan served us Ben & Jerry's Ice Cream, of which he had a lifetime supply to honor his life of activism.

I'm not sure John has an ice cream named after him yet, but he probably will. John's written dozens of books, and hundreds of articles. He was nominated for the Nobel Peace Prize by none other than the late Archbishop Desmond

Tutu. Not all of us can say that. But I don't feel like I need to give you a full biography or embarrass him any more—he's one of the most humble people I know.

Here's what I want to say. John Dear is a force for love. He is fuelled by his love for Jesus, his love for life; even his love for his enemies.

John Dear is a troublemaker. The best kind of troublemaker. He's been arrested over 80 times, so his record speaks for itself... literally. But he doesn't just have a criminal record; he is leaving behind a legacy of love and justice.

John's got that fire in his bones that the prophets had— that doesn't allow him to accept the world as it is, or defend the status quo. It pushes him to imagine the world as it could be—as it should be. He has a deep, intimate love for Jesus that oozes out of him. He has a contagious joy that rubs off on you.

But let there be no mistake. John Dear is a divine rebel. He makes the devil nervous. And he keeps the FBI busy, keeping his files up to date.

John and I have gone to jail together. He's been arrested a few more times than me; but he also has a few years on me, so I might catch up. We've prayed together, wept together, laughed until we wheezed together.

We went to Afghanistan together, to visit a group of young people who share our passion for nonviolence. It was an incredible experience, but one of the things I remember most was watching John listen—intently listen—to these teenagers talk about their dreams for a world free of war and violence. And then, in characteristic contagious wonder he kept saying: "They read Dr. King—in Farsi—*in Farsi* Shane. And they are 15 years old!"

As I flipped the pages of this book, I was reminded that our community, The Simple Way, began as an act of civil disobedience. A group of fearless, homeless mothers moved into an abandoned Catholic church. It was an act of survival, but it was also an act of civil disobedience. They were threatened with arrest by the Catholic Archdiocese for sleeping in an abandoned sanctuary.

They hung a banner on the front of the church that said: *How can we worship a homeless man on Sunday and ignore one on Monday?* They held a press conference and announced: "We mean no disrespect to the Catholic officials, but we have talked with the real Owner of this building... and God said that we can stay." These mothers and children were walking in the same tradition as the prophets and revolutionaries. That's how it all started for us: civil disobedience.

As we started our community here on the north side of Philadelphia over 20 years ago, around the corner from the old abandoned church, I remember reading Henry Thoreau's 1849 essay on Civil Disobedience. It helped ground me in the rich tradition of nonviolent direct action.

Then I moved on to Jacques Ellul's *Anarchy and Christianity* and Vernard Eller's *Christian Anarchy*, and then Leo Tolstoy and Dorothy Day's many books, and Dan Berrigan's Poems. All of them called us not to conform to the world around us. As Paul writes in Romans: "Do not conform to the patterns of this world... but be transformed by the renewing of your mind." Live with imagination. Don't accept the world as it is; dream of the world as it should be.

Thoreau's essay was invigorating, and so are the classics. But we need a fresh look at what Civil Disobedience means for us today. A manifesto for what John Lewis called "good trouble". Now we have it. In fact, we had it before, but now we have it updated, and back in print.

In this book, John has added to the library—to the Holy Mischief section. John reminds us that there is a rich tradition of civil disobedience in the Christian faith, and many other faith traditions as well. Moses's birth was an act of civil disobedience. The entire narrative of Exodus is the story of God liberating the Hebrew people from the crushing force of slavery in Pharaoh's empire.

Weaved all through Scripture are stories of civil disobedience: Shadrach, Meshach and Abednego thrown into the fiery furnace. Daniel thrown in the lion's den. Jeremiah jailed. John the Baptist beheaded. Philemon welcoming a fugitive slave as a brother; Paul and Silas busted out of prison by an act of God. Jesus making a spectacle of the system of death as he hung on the cross, God's love on full display. The Bible is a revolutionary book. And Christians have frequented jails over and over throughout the centuries.

But this is not just a book about theory or history; this is a handbook for revolution. This is a reminder that we need to raise up a new generation of holy troublemakers today— troublemakers deeply grounded in love and committed to nonviolence. Rosa Parks and Harriet Tubman are not just icons of history; they inspire us to be courageous in our own way. Their courage is contagious. We think of Colin Kaepernick taking a knee in the national anthem, and Bree Newsome taking down the Confederate flag in front of the South Carolina Capitol. Courage comes in many different shapes and forms. And we need courage today to challenge the "principalities and powers" that are crushing people's lives; we need courage to defend the planet itself against those who ruthlessly exploit it for profit.

John has taught me this: love is a cantankerous thing. Love is kind and gentle sometimes. But love is also offensive, disruptive, uncomfortable. Jesus wept over Jerusalem, but he also flipped tables in the Temple. That's the love Dostoevsky spoke of; not the sentimental love of fairytales and romance novels, but the love that love can get you in trouble. It can get you put in jail. It can get you killed. It was that kind of love that landed Jesus on the cross. It was that kind of love that got Dr. King killed, and Gandhi killed. And so many others. So be forewarned—this book is dangerous. It will probably get added to some of the banned book lists that many prisons have, and now many schools have. But this book is about truth, and love; daredevil love.

And as you will see, this book is not so much about civil disobedience, but divine obedience. It is our holy, God-ordained duty to challenge the bad laws as much as it is our duty to uphold the good ones. As St. Augustine said, "An unjust law is no law at all." Gandhi and King taught us that "noncooperation with evil is as much a duty as cooperation with good."

I remember hearing that Dr. King once expressed a bit of discomfort about going to jail—but then he looked at history, and saw what good company he had: all the saints and history makers who found themselves in jail. It was King, of course, who said, "There is nothing wrong with a traffic law which says you should stop at a red light... but when a fire is raging, the fire truck goes right through the red light." There is a fire raging today—many fires, and lives are at stake. That's why we need this book.

Of course, when someone lobbed an insult at Dr. King saying that he was "maladjusted", he took the insult and embraced it, insisting that we live in a world that has become way too adjusted to injustice, way to adjusted to racism, and violence, and war, and poverty and all sorts of evil. We need some holy maladjusted people. This book invites you to be maladjusted in the best kind of way.

It is this prophetic imagination that inspired Peter Maurin, co-founder of the Catholic Worker movement alongside Dorothy Day. When someone said Peter was "crazy", he had the best retort: "If I am crazy, it is because I refuse to be crazy in the same way the world has gone crazy."

John Dear is one of the wild folks who refuses to normalize injustice. He laughs at the lies of our materialistic world, trying to convince us that happiness must be purchased or that we can bomb our way to peace. John Dear has the audacity to believe the world can be different—that we can be different.

My hope is that you will read this book and find firm footing for a life of holy trouble. If love does ever land you in jail, you'll be reminded of what good company you have behind bars. And if love ever costs you your life, you can stand confidently on the promise that we will rise again. As the old saying goes, "They tried to bury us, but they didn't know that we were seeds."

This book is a gift to the world. And so is John Dear.

— *Shane Claiborne*

Author, activist, co-founder of
Red Letter Christians

Introduction

(adapted from 1994 edition)

God is constantly at work in us, and in our world, bringing forth God's reign of justice and peace on earth, here and now, as it is in heaven. Nonviolent civil disobedience is one way for us to cooperate with God's nonviolent, loving transformation of our world. When nonviolent civil disobedience is enacted in the Spirit of God's love—as an act of obedience to the God of nonviolent love—it can be a force for the transformation of the world; it becomes sacramental.

The term "sacrament" will be unfamiliar to some. It emerged through the centuries to signify those life-giving, graced moments when God is intensely present in ordinary experiences of human life—and where, in return, the community of Christ collectively affirms what it is, and aspires to be.[1] Jesus certainly did not leave a well-defined set of sacramental rituals in his teachings,* but even the early Christian community had a sense of sacramental acts; for example, washing each others' feet, preaching, speaking

---

* In the Eastern Orthodox and Roman Catholic traditions, the term "sacrament" has come to refer exclusively, since the middle ages, to seven liturgical rites: baptism, confirmation, eucharist, penance, anointing of the sick, marriage, and orders.

in tongues, prophesying, healing, and praying—particularly the laying of hands on another person, as a way to pass on the Spirit of Jesus.

I believe that, when rooted in faith, the act of nonviolent civil disobedience is an experience of the sacred. Certainly it is an event filled with both mystery and meaning. If we act with predisposed, open, loving hearts, then we will experience the grace of God's spirit working through us. We may not fully understand what is happening, but we will sense that God is present. At most, we may feel the consolation of God's own peace; a great gift indeed.

Civil disobedience, when enacted with a spirit of prayerful, nonviolent love, can be both a sign and the reality—the *sacramentum et res*—of Christ's love, present and transforming and overcoming evil through his body, the Christian community. It marks a sacred reality, and thus sanctifies not only the people engaged in it, but those who witness it and are the focus of it. It is both a symbol and an act of transformation; an invitation to the transformation we seek, and the transformation that is already happening in us and in the world through the loving Spirit of God. It is an act of self-transcendence, because it reveals who we are becoming: a nonviolent, peacemaking people, followers of Jesus, who love their enemies, forgive others, and seek the truth of justice for the poor.

Though we will probably not know the 'effect' of our symbolic activity, the felt presence of God's love in this process will sustain us to trust in God with real hope and to continue along the Way of the Gospels. In this spirit, our action will bear the fruit of peace in ways we never dreamed—perhaps for generations to come—because God will be at the heart of the action. Like the witness of Dr. King, Dorothy Day, and others since, our sacramental deeds may secure a more just and peaceful future and inspire unborn generations to walk in the Way of nonviolent love.

Disobedience in the face of disaster

Civil disobedience is not the only way to resist injustice; it is not the only way to be faithful to the God of peace, and the peacemaking Christ. But in these days of rampant poverty, climate catastrophe and nuclear madness, it is becoming more and more necessary for some of us as Christians to stand up and risk our reputations, our freedom, even our lives, to say *NO* to death in all its forms, and *YES* to the sacred gift of life; and to do this through public acts of nonviolent civil disobedience.

Social transformation, in other words, requires that people break the laws which legalize injustice and ecocide, and accept the consequences of their peaceful actions. This dynamic of peaceful resistance and voluntary suffering opens the door to a new world of justice and peace.

In 2018, I wrote about the many interconnections between the difficulties that we now face:

Today, we wage some thirty wars; possess some 10,000 nuclear weapons; and allow unparalleled corporate greed and economic inequality—along with the extreme poverty that entails for over three billion people. We maintain a global epidemic of violence, rooted in racism, sexism and the oppression of the poor and disenfranchised. With our global rejection of Jesus' way of nonviolence, and our global pursuit of nature's resources at any expense, we have reversed the direction of creation and set off catastrophic climate change.

Gas emissions, temperatures and sea levels have risen dramatically and extreme weather now threatens us all. With the fossil fuel industry digging up the earth, as well as the methane released by cattle who are being fattened for America's meat industry, we are filling the atmosphere with carbon. Temperatures rise; the ice caps melt; the seas rise; the storms get bigger; and the violent reaction of Mother Earth begins.

We have bulldozed the forests and the Amazon, harvested the ocean of its fish, destroyed the soil and the vegetation, killed the coral reefs and poisoned the waters. We are killing the earth; but it will not go down without a fight. Total catastrophic climate violence is the normal, predictable scientific response. Scientists predict a hundred new wars over water and land during this century (the current war in Ukraine is an obvious example).

Hundreds of millions may be forced to flee their homes; at least 250 million new refugees by 2050. Nearly every person will live in poverty, because of the loss of liveable land and drinking water. Billions will die needlessly; many more will suffer. Scientists describe a hellish reality that is hard to imagine, but inevitable unless drastic changes are made immediately.[2]

Already, we see how prolonged drought, continuous flooding and the ravages of uncontrollable forest fires are leading to the migration of peoples from south to north—and the inability of the rich world to cope, beyond building walls and mobilising the military to keep these migrants out.[*] Yet the avoidance of debate, let alone action, with regard to the evils of the global economy—especially its causal relationship with climate breakdown and environmental destruction—is ubiquitous.

In other words, violence is not abating in the world, but is instead worsening. So it is necessary for us to reflect anew on our nonviolent civil disobedience so that we might become *more* nonviolent, *more* civil, and *more* disobedient to the forces of violence and death which are killing the human family; indeed, so that we might become more obedient to the God of justice and nonviolent love, and thus be instruments of God's transforming love.

Sacramental civil disobedience by the community of believers addresses the world with a message of peace: the peace that has already been granted to us by God and the reconciliation already given to humanity through the life, death and resurrection of Christ. Civil disobedience can be a public, symbolic ceremony which proclaims that peace—even to the point of arrest, imprisonment, persecution and death if necessary—so that Jesus' Way of redemptive suffering love may become reality.

—

[*] Since most of the countries currently affected by climate change are inhabited by people of colour, the Black Lives Matter campaign, sparked by the murder of George Floyd in Minneapolis, has a profound connection with climate crisis protests.

In this way, sacramental civil disobedience can even become a spiritual 'rite of passage' as it marks our movement into the realm of public dissent from the policies of injustice and war. It is a paradigm of *all* resistance and protest to whatever is dehumanizing, unjust, violent, deadly, or ungodly. It models our divine obedience, and demonstrates a way that humans can live out the ideals of love, justice, and peace on the societal level. In doing so, it shows the world how to confront injustice and war by transforming it with God's active love and truth.

We could call this witness the sacrament of prayerful protest, the sacrament of speaking truth to power, the sacrament of nonviolent resistance to evil, or the sacrament of civil disobedience; but however we articulate the movement of the spirit, we know that we are simply trying to fulfill our duties as followers of Jesus. We are trying to overcome evil through the goodness of nonviolent love, as Jesus did; to shed the light of truth amid the darkness of our warring world; to cross the line which defends the horrors of injustice of all kinds in a profound act of love and divine obedience.

More people, including more Christians, have been arrested in acts of nonviolent civil disobedience in recent years than ever before; and yet there are few books on the meaning of civil disobedience. The radical nonviolence and civil disobedience of the early Christians has been neglected through centuries of 'blessing the Empire'; but perhaps now, in our own day and age, we have the graced opportunity to reclaim that same illegal fidelity in our tradition through sacramental, nonviolent direct action as a response to the violence of the times and the love of God inviting us to make peace.

I write from the perspective of a white, middle class, North American Catholic who has been arrested and jailed some eighty-five times for acts of nonviolent civil disobedience across the country: at the White House and the Pentagon; at the Trident submarine base in St. Mary's Georgia and at West Point in New York; at the Federal Building in Los Angeles, the Army's West Coast Presidio in San Francisco and the Strategic Air Command Center outside of Omaha, Nebraska.

The actions I've taken, the trials and experiences of jail—with its confinement, living solidarity with the poor, bible study, and daily Eucharist—have been for me a great grace, a deep blessing, an experience of God. Our action was indeed sacramental. It has been a sharing in the paschal mystery of Christ. To that end, I believe, it will bear good fruit for the God of peace.

Civil disobedience undoubtedly risks and entails painful consequences, as the life of Jesus makes clear. But suffering, arrests, jail, torture, and death were the common fate of the early Christians and remain today a real possibility for the faithful still in many parts of the world. We too are now willing to risk these consequences for the sake of the reign of God, for suffering humanity, and for our commitment to the Gospel.

I do not propose to offer conclusive answers to people's questions; in fact, the book may only raise more of them. I do hope, however, that this book may help further discussion and reflection in the Christian community and beyond, as we seek to live out our calling to be peacemakers within a warmaking society and within a culture of unparalleled violence.

We are all still learning the depths of the nonviolence which we are called to explore; what it means to follow the peacemaking Jesus, to know what that first community knew in their constant struggle for truth and love in the public forum. While this may be new and dangerous ground for many of us, it is exciting and uplifting nevertheless. In order to practice this public, sacramental nonviolence in acts of civil disobedience, we must be prepared.

PART ONE:

Our
Tradition of
Disobedience

ONE

A Different Way is Possible

Expressing obedience to God's law

One New York winter evening in the early 1980s, a small peace group gathered for a regular Bible study meeting; when word came of an insidious deed waged upon the homeless. A prestigious library in the center of Manhattan had placed barbed wire on the heating grates around its building, to keep homeless people away. We were dumbfounded; aghast at this callous behavior. Most of us in our little group worked with homeless people: serving in soup kitchens; volunteering and coordinating night shelters; offering hospitality as we could; seeking affordable housing for others; and speaking out against the militarism which causes homelessness. We knew that the homeless suffer on the front lines of a war waged against the poor, and this latest development symbolized society's effort to push the homeless out of sight.

"There is only one thing we can do," Daniel Berrigan calmly suggested. "Cut the wire." It was as simple as that.

We nodded our approval and stood up to close the meeting. We joined hands and bowed our heads in a moment of silent prayer. The following week, just two days before Christmas, thirty of us gathered in front of the library. A contingent of representatives went inside the building to speak with the library officials. The rest of us broke into cheerful Christmas carols.

Our negotiators returned. No, the library would not remove the barbed wire, we were told. Wire-cutters were produced. Several of us proceeded to cut the barbed wire. Shortly afterwards, police cars appeared. We lined the sidewalk along the building.

A complaint had been issued. Questions were raised. Who had cut the wire? Who had destroyed private property? Who had committed the crime?

Indeed. Who *had* committed the crime?

We joined hands and broke into Christmas song. The thirty of us stood singing. The police paced back and forth. After a while, they left. No charges were pressed.

Ours was a humble act, but it sent a signal: putting up barbed wire is a barbarous activity and would not be tolerated. We knew from harsh reality that we could not solve all the problems of the homeless; we could not find homes for everyone. The crisis is too large for a handful of concerned folk. But our little group could take a stand on their behalf, in their struggle for justice. We could do something on this specific, symbolic point which said so much about society's attitude towards the homeless.

The stand was taken; the wire was cut. It was never replaced.

Nonviolent direct action

Throughout history, concerned people have stood up for the cause of justice, for the sake of suffering humanity, risking their lives in the process. More and more people today are realizing the need to stand up to the widespread injustice and mass violence committed by governments and military forces throughout the world. More and more people are pointing out to governments their failure to take effective action to prevent the climate emergency.

People are beginning to understand the truth of reality. As many as 15,000 human beings die of starvation every day; over two-thirds of the world lives in dire poverty; 37.2 million US citizens live below the poverty line; and with only 4.25% percent of the world's population, the United States consumes nearly 16% percent of the world's resources.

Racism, sexism, torture, and other forms of violence have been institutionalized as normative; nearly 30 wars are currently being waged on the planet and those wars are supported, at least through the sale of weapons, by the United States; the world still has over 13,000 nuclear weapons, enough to destroy the planet perhaps 130 times over; one US or UK Trident submarine alone carries twenty-five times the destructive force of World War II—and the US has a fleet of 14 Trident submarines.

Every day, people are waking up to the realization that we, in the West, are responsible for these horrors and that we need to resist these injustices. What should a conscientious Christ follower do, living in a society which practices rampant injustice, wages war on the poor at home and abroad, and over-consumes the natural resources of the planet as if we had one and three quarter planets to plunder for profit? How are we to resist the forces of death around us?

After prayer and reflection on the realities of war, injustice, violence, inequality nuclear holocaust and the impending climate catastrophe, many Christians have entered into symbolic, nonviolent direct action for peace and justice. They are trying to enter into God's transformation of evil into good. They desire to be faithful to the actively nonviolent peacemaking of Jesus.

Cutting barbed wire is just one small example of what is usually called nonviolent direct action, or civil disobedience. When Mohandas K. Gandhi, India's apostle of nonviolence, picked up a handful of salt from the sea on April 6, 1930, he broke the law and sent forth an electric spirit among the masses, which eventually forced the British to leave India.

December 1, 1955: When Rosa Parks refused to give up her seat on a segregated bus in Montgomery, Alabama, she broke the law and was arrested for her action; she sparked the brewing struggle for civil rights into a full-fledged movement that captured the attention of the world.

When a little band of resisters, including a woman named Dorothy Day, sat in a New York City park to protest nuclear war defense drills, they broke the law and unmasked the lie that nuclear war is winnable.

May 19, 1968: When Daniel and Philip Berrigan entered the Knights of Columbus Hall in Catonsville, Maryland, removed draft files and burned them with napalm, they broke the law and set in motion a string of similar protests against the Vietnam war, helping to end it.

September 9, 1980: When the Berrigans and their friends entered the General Electric nuclear weapons plant in King of Prussia, Pennsylvania, and hammered on a nuclear missile nosecone, they broke the law and inspired scores of others to take similar action to beat nuclear 'swords' into 'plowshares' of peace.

May 25th, 2020: When George Floyd was murdered by a state police officer in Mineapolis, a new, more determined movement was born, to protest the profound inequalities experienced along race lines in every society throughout the world.

When Jim and Shelley Douglass and the members of the Ground Zero community sat on the tracks in front of the nuclear 'white train,' which carried more explosive power than all the weapons fired in World War II, they broke the law and encouraged a wave of nonviolent tracksitters to block the train as it crisscrossed the country, uncovering the nuclear nightmare passing through every backyard of nearly every US neighborhood.

When the black community in South Africa overran a segregated 'whites only' beach and dove into the ocean for a swim, they broke the law, risking arrest and execution; their nonviolent civil disobedience served to speed up the end of apartheid.

When a handful of peace activists drove their motorized rubber raft in front of a Trident Submarine preparing to launch a Trident D-5 missile—perhaps the most lethal weapon ever created—they broke the law and inspired others to protest the testing, production and use of nuclear weapons.

September 2019: Many broke the law when, it was estimated, more than 250,000 people turned out for protests in New York against Government inaction on climate change, with thousands more demonstrating in Boston, Miami and San Francisco.

•

Positive social change only occurs in history when good people break bad laws and accept the consequences. When such stands are taken, the nonviolent transformation of our world is sparked anew. God's reign of nonviolent love breaks through our world again. Such actions help us to remember that we are all sisters and brothers, children of a loving God who calls us to love one another and to live together in peace with justice for all.

Nonviolent civil disobedience can take a variety of forms and is only limited to the creative energies of our imagination. On one occasion, members of the Community for Creative Nonviolence in Washington, DC joined the daily tour of the White House. Once inside the State Dining Room, they let loose hundreds of cockroaches to symbolize not only the plight of the inner city poor (who suffer from plagues of cockroaches), but the fact that no one will survive a nuclear war except, scientists say, the cockroach. Those cockroaches scattered in every direction across that dining room floor, disappearing into the marrow of the building.

The resisters were arrested; they had graphically pointed out the realities of poverty and nuclearism.

On another occasion, housing activists from the South, gathering on the grounds of the US Capitol, let loose twenty chickens on the Capitol lawn. The activists then unfurled a banner which read, "Money for Housing is Chicken Feed."

Guards at the Electric Boat Trident nuclear submarine plant in Groton, Connecticut were surprised one Christmas Eve morning to find a score of Santa Clauses dressed in their red uniforms, black belts, and white beards, blocking the entrance way. The hilarious Santa Claus action caught the attention of the whole state, and raised a very Christian question: how can we celebrate Christmas while we continue to plan the destruction of the planet and the human race?

When a student peace group at a Catholic university realized the school was permitting a recruiter from the CIA (with its notorious record of violence, terrorism, and assassination) to interview students on campus, they sat-in and blocked the doorways to the meeting area in the Dean's office. Within the hour, the university asked the CIA recruiter to leave.

Nonviolent civil disobedience can be defined in many ways. Some understand it simply as an extreme form of dissent. Others characterize civil disobedience as active, public resistance to evil, whether that evil be war, nuclearism or some other specific injustice. Such disobedience usually breaks an unjust law—or the laws which defend an unjust status quo. It includes accepting the consequences of one's action, including the possibility of imprisonment or death. It can be practiced individually, or by large groups.

It is, in other words, the public act of standing up and nonviolently protesting some societal evil, come what may. It puts into practice our responsibility to challenge injustice, by speaking the truth about justice and peace and by putting our bodies and spirits on the line. It is a public, nonviolent confrontation of the nation-state systems which dominate and oppress human life. As such, nonviolent civil disobedience is a way to change the world into a more just, more peaceful place for everyone. It is a way to cooperate with God's redemptive love and truth—which is already at work actively transforming human hearts, nations and the whole world into a realm of nonviolent justice and peace.

Beyond just and unjust laws

The term 'civil disobedience' was originally coined by Henry David Thoreau, the nineteenth century naturalist and essayist, most famous for his book *Walden*. In 1846, after reflecting on the US war with Mexico and the evils of slavery, Thoreau decided not to pay the annual poll tax, as a simple protest to systemic violence and injustice.

He was arrested and jailed overnight. Subsequently, he wrote about the need to oppose the immoral activity of governments. His 1849 essay, *Resistance to Civil Government**, challenges readers to resist injustice actively,

---

* Later titled *On the Duty of Civil Disobedience.*

and to overcome evil with goodness—even if that means undergoing suffering, getting arrested, and going to jail. "Under a government which imprisons anyone unjustly," Thoreau concluded, "the true place for a just person is also a prison."

The practice of nonviolent direct action, Thoreau believed, spelled the end of injustice. Yes, it would take time, he knew, but the demise of the injustice, the war, the violence, was guaranteed:

> If one *honest* person, in this State of Massachusetts, ceasing to hold slaves, were actually to withdraw from this copartnership, and be locked up in the county jail therefore, it would be the abolition of slavery in America. For it matters not how small the beginning may seem to be: what is once well done, is done for ever.[1]

Thoreau understood the power of truth against systemic injustice, when put into practice through active, nonviolent, civil disobedience. Good fruit, as Jesus said, always comes forth from good actions.

Thoreau's philosophy of life left a deep impression on many peacemakers—most notably, Gandhi. Through Gandhi, and then Martin Luther King Jr., Dorothy Day and many others, civil disobedience has become a standard tool for the pursuit of justice and peace.

Over the decades, civil disobedience has been redefined as the breaking of an *unjust civil law* in obedience to a *higher law*, sometimes with the hope of changing the unjust civil law.[2] Martin Luther King Jr. distinguished these two types of laws in his *Letter from a Birmingham Jail*—written, as the title suggests, while imprisoned for eight days following his civil disobedience in the Alabama civil rights campaign.

To a group of white clergymen, he describes a moral responsibility both to obey *just* laws, but to disobey *unjust* laws, recalling St. Augustine's comment that "an unjust law is no law at all."[3] We might today call them 'pro-human' and 'anti-human' laws: does a law serve humanity—*all* humanity—or does it bring suffering and death to humanity, to even one person? Does it help everyone, or does it hurt anyone—even just one person?

Laws which encourage people to drive carefully under a certain speed limit; to avoid littering; to stop at traffic lights; to enable postal service; to facilitate waste and garbage disposal; to protect swimmers in the ocean or pools—these are helpful to humanity, assuming that violators are treated nonviolently, and that oppression of minorities does not occur. The Nuremberg principles which outlaw genocide, human rights violations and other injustices, uphold the sanctity of life and justice. As long as such laws stay within God's higher law of nonviolent love, they can be helpful.

When the law is used to defend systemic injustice—to allow a handful of rich people to control the resources of the world, and to support the oppression of masses of impoverished people—then the law is misused and becomes 'anti-human.' Philip Berrigan writes:

When law does not uncompromisingly uphold human life as sacred, when it makes no provision for conscience and love of enemies, when it does not protect and rescue the weak and helpless (the state would evaporate if it did; so would the state's law), then it is social and political sin, a subtle and deviant curse, deserving only to be resisted and broken.[4]

With the advent of the climate emergency, we have even discovered how the *absence* of law, where law is needed, can be equally anti-human too. Most countries are in retreat from their legal obligations under the 2015 Paris Agreement. Laws have either not been framed, are wholly inadequate or are not being adhered to. Such abnegation of responsibility by the state, in the face of such threats to the wellbeing of both human and non-human populations of the planet, plays a part in the systemic violence that calls for civil disobedience.

Like Berrigan, though, many have asked whether a nonviolent, just society is even possible, with the state in its current form. As more people begin to critique the systems which legally support racism, sexism, war, nuclearism, hunger, and poverty—systems which make minor reforms in the name of legalism and justice, but which continue to oppress and kill—they are naturally asking whether laws *can* truly be rooted in nonviolence; whether they can be 'pro-human'.

Framing our discussion in terms of 'the law'—the traditional understanding of civil disobedience—implies a basic faith in the system itself; a desire merely to reform the system, instead of transforming it. One disobeys unjust laws, the theory goes, in order to make changes on the level of consciousness, and then in the law itself. But this definition of civil disobedience fails to address the root evils of the system itself, and the need for an entirely new way of life.

In the US, as peace activist Elizabeth McAlister explains, the Constitution and the Bill of Rights "speak of government and citizens as if they constituted the whole calculus," whereas the true forces and powers that control policies, and govern the economy, are far less quantifiable or accountable—the Pentagon, the CIA, NSA, and "gigantic transnational corporations":

> These have, for longer than we've known, shaped the world into rich and poor, privileged and oppressed. We do not do civil disobedience so much as we engage in symbolic action to witness to the truth about our lives today. We believe that restoring symbols and purifying them through suffering and public exposure are part of the renewal of a *community of sanity*, which ought to be the definition of the church.[5]

In this light, nonviolent civil disobedience is defined as a symbolic way to confront systemic violence with a loving witness to the truth: God's truth of nonviolence. Thomas Merton, the Trappist monk and peacemaker, wrote that nonviolent civil disobedience touches the deepest levels in humanity when it is rooted in God and enacted in response to the Spirit of Peace transforming the world.

"The whole point of nonviolence," Merton wrote shortly before his death in 1968, "is that it rises above pragmatism and does not consider whether or not it pays off politically. *Ahimsa* [nonviolence] is defense of and witness to truth, not efficacy."[6]

Merton tried diligently to keep the movement of nonviolent resistance rooted in love, humility, dialogue, repentance, prayer, contemplation, and respect for others. He did not want people acting simply to get on the nightly news. As Gordan Zahn has written, "For Merton, acts of civil disobedience were the means by which the truth that can save us is to be achieved if it is to be achieved at all. The great need is to discover the form of civil disobedience that is most appropriate to a given place and time."[7]

Dorothy Day, the founder of the Catholic Worker, was a regular practitioner of nonviolent civil disobedience to state-sanctioned violence. She saw her life as a constant battle with what she called "this filthy rotten system." She insisted that her acts of nonviolent civil disobedience were part of a lived continuum; part of a whole lifestyle of protest, which included prayer, Bible study, receiving the sacraments, serving the poor, offering hospitality to the homeless, speaking out on issues of justice, writing, voluntary poverty, constructive work, and community living.

For Day, nonviolent civil disobedience was one significant ingredient in a lifelong discipleship to the peacemaking Jesus. It was a public way for her to challenge the system of violence. During the Vietnam war, her advice to young

Catholics was short and to the point: "We should fill the jails with young people who refuse to fight."

As Martin Luther King Jr. practiced nonviolent civil disobedience—undergoing arrest nineteen times during his short life—his understanding of civil disobedience developed. During his steadfast campaign for civil rights, King's civil disobedience was an effort to reform the nation-state system, not to break beyond it or transform it. He lobbied Congress and the White House to change the legal structures which supported injustice.

In the late 1960s, though, King began to see that the system itself was so rooted in injustice that it had to be changed. In 1966, he began to grope for a new vision beyond the present militaristic structures of the US government, discussing with his friends what nonviolent, democratic socialism might look like in the United States. He wanted to see the birth of a new world order of nonviolence, where the poor would be fed and housed, and wars would no longer be prepared for or supported.

In the last two years of his life, Dr. King began to realize a need to go beyond the traditional understanding of civil disobedience. He started to explore the possibility that fidelity to the Gospel of Christ requires nonviolent civil disobedience to systemic evil. With his public denunciation of the Vietnam war, his thinking deepened. King traveled across the country, in his last year of life, calling for "a radical revolution of values." Over and over again, he drew the same conclusion:

Our only hope today lies in our ability to recapture the revolutionary spirit and go out into a sometimes hostile world declaring eternal hostility to poverty, racism, and militarism. With this powerful commitment we shall boldly challenge the status quo and unjust mores and thereby speed the day when 'every valley shall be exalted, and every mountain and hill shall be made low, and the crooked shall be made straight and the rough places plain'... This call for a world-wide fellowship that lifts neighborly concern beyond one's tribe, race, class and nation is in reality a call for an all-embracing and unconditional love for all men and women.[8]

In the end, Dr. King called for massive civil disobedience by hundreds of thousands of impoverished people, in a long-term campaign scheduled to take place in Washington, DC, in the summer of 1968. The Poor People's Campaign had the potential to become a nonviolent revolution which could set in motion the transformation King dreamed of. In the past, he had targeted specific cities across the country for reform—from Montgomery and Birmingham to Chicago and Memphis. Now his work in Washington, DC was aimed at radically transforming the US government itself, and thus the nation as a whole.

It was at this point in his life quest that he was assassinated. His challenge was so serious, the potential for transformation so great, that the forces of death he so diligently resisted killed him to prevent that transformation from occurring. We are left today not only to ponder in what direction Dr. King might have gone, but to take up where he left off.

Dorothy Day and Dr. King realized that the duty of the Christian was not to offer a five year plan, a final solution, or some new system to replace the old. Rather, they understood that the Christian simply offers the vision of the Gospel, a world where everyone loves everyone else as their own sister or brother. They understood that the vision of Jesus was not a military strategy but a way of life. Jesus rooted his vision in freedom and nonviolent love, and proclaimed God's reign of nonviolence. Day, King and others have taken seriously Jesus' proclamation, for they know that this reign of nonviolent love is the only hope for the world.

The focus of civil disobedience, then, is not solely on breaking the law or getting arrested. The focus is the Gospel vision of God's reconciliation and justice. The focal point is the proclamation of the reign of God and its transforming Spirit. In this newer understanding of nonviolent civil disobedience, our *obedience to God* becomes the reason for our action. The task at hand is to do what is right, to proclaim the higher law and its implications for justice and peace, here and now. Civil disobedience, therefore, is a public, active way to express our obedience to God's law of nonviolent love and justice.

As people called to obey God's law of nonviolent love— and as practitioners of that law—we do not support violence, whether that be the mass murder of warfare, the institutionalized violence of poverty and hunger, or the systemic degradation of the ecological systems that sustain us. We follow Jesus, the gentle revolutionary who confronted every facet of violence with a transforming spirit of nonviolent love.

Like the obedient Jesus, we proclaim God's reign of nonviolent love. His challenge to the legal system of imperial violence, and its flipside of religious oppression (symbolized in the Temple), resulted first of all in his crucifixion. But his subsequent resurrection was the fruit of his deep nonviolence, his fidelity and his obedience to God, and it paved the way for generations of nonviolent people to be born.

We Christians are called to rediscover ourselves as a people who hold allegiance only to God; as a people who practice, proclaim and promote God's way of nonviolent love and justice for all.

We are no longer a people who pledge allegiance solely to any nation, empire or worldly power, to any organization rooted in violence. Christians are citizens of the reign of God, and thus, our identity goes beyond limited categories such as Democrat or Republican, communist, capitalist or imperialist, conservative or liberal. Sometimes, our proclamation takes the form of nonviolent civil disobedience. We disobey the rules which govern the reign of violence and injustice. We obey God and God's rule of love and thus enter into God's transformation of the world.

To participate in God's transformation of our world, our actions need to reflect God's transforming love. "Civil disobedience done with love," theologian and activist Jim Douglass writes, "rather than the intention of acting against someone, is a deeply liberating force":

> The more loving an act of civil disobedience is, the more powerful it will be. Loving disobedience says in action that God alone is sovereign, and that the blasphemous securities of our lives and nation must be surrendered for the sake of life.[9]

This life of loving disobedience to the systems of violence is a life of loving *obedience* to the God of nonviolent love, justice and peace. It is an invitation to take concrete steps into the reign of God, and away from the reign of violence and systemic injustice.

To clarify our understanding of civil disobedience to law and divine obedience to God's love, it may be helpful to turn next to the Hebrew and Christian scriptures, and to learn from our biblical ancestors.

TWO

We Will Not Serve Your False God

The Biblical roots of civil disobedience

In the early 1980s, I witnessed my friends under arrest for speaking out against the nuclear policies of the nation. The sight set me on a course of deep meditation and reflection; a course that could only lead to nonviolent action. The many others who had, for decades, 'kept vigil' at the Pentagon— who demonstrated for peace, spoke with employees, and blocked doorways in protest and hope—had touched me with their transforming spirit. Thus several months later, I joined in that tradition of active peacemaking by sitting-in at the Pentagon myself.

I was arrested, handcuffed, briefly jailed, tried in the federal court—and deeply moved by the Spirit of Peace that touched me throughout the experience. The nonviolent resistance of Dorothy Day, Martin Luther King Jr., Gandhi and other models of peacemaking had long exemplified the way I wanted to live my own life; I had meditated daily on the peacemaking ministry of Jesus; but I had only begun to grasp the roots of nonviolent civil disobedience which go back to the earliest days of human history. Although it was not called 'civil disobedience' in ancient times, people have been illegally resisting the legal evils of the world for thousands of years. Civil disobedience, in other words, has biblical roots.

The book of Hebrews calls attention to these inspiring roots by listing an array of Jewish ancestors who comprise a veritable "cloud of witnesses," urging us on, encouraging Christians to be faithful to the troublemaking way of Jesus; those who "did what was just... endured mockery, scourging, even chains and imprisonment." (Hebrews 11:32-38).

Such noble people obeyed God and risked their lives by disobeying the imperial idols who demanded obedience and violence. As the writer concludes: "The world was not worthy of them." Yet we do not always read the Hebrew Scriptures as the stories of illegal, provocative actions undertaken in obedience to God, in defiance of the ruling authorities of the day.

A serious study of nonviolent civil disobedience in the Hebrew Scriptures has yet to be written; and there is so much history, so much power in these narratives, that it is presumptuous to attempt a definitive overview, analysis or reflection on these texts in a short chapter. For our purposes, though, I will review a few selected passages to highlight the roots of the biblical call to peacemaking which urges us on today. It was stories such as these that inspired Jesus to pursue public actions on behalf of the reign of God.

The Hebrew Scriptures focus on such themes as liberation, justice, the law, faithfulness to God, idolatry, and a strong condemnation of nations and empires.

Various prophets appear throughout the text to announce a message from God. Their words of truth urge people to do God's will: to pursue justice and peace, and to abandon their foolish idolatries or violent systems of death.

According to the vision of the prophets, fidelity to God's covenant of justice and peace can often require disobeying and opposing the military-imperial forces which wage war and oppress the poor. From Elijah to Jeremiah, God's prophets faced opposition from the rulers of their day, and received frequent death threats. Yet they refused to bend to the caprices of the authorities. They stubbornly obeyed God, and insisted that others do so as well. More often than not, they were killed for their provocative, holy truth-telling. Such talk took many forms, but it was invariably 'civilly disobedient.'

These stories of resistance include the apocalyptic, visionary book of Daniel; the most explicit account of nonviolent civil disobedience in the Hebrew Scriptures. Centuries later, the first evangelist, the author of the Gospel of Mark, cited every chapter of the book of Daniel—more than any other scripture text—in his effort to tell the story of Jesus' campaign of revolutionary nonviolence. Jesus, it would appear, modeled himself on the radical vision and nonviolence of Daniel.

A brief overview of some of these prophetic texts to which Jesus may have turned, especially in the book of Daniel, may help us in our own discernment of nonviolent civil disobedience.

Stories of nonviolent non-cooperation with evil

Theologian and activist Ched Myers writes that the "political tactic" of civil disobedience did not exist as we know it in the Hebrew world. Kings in the ancient Mediterranean world would be seen as divine, Myers notes; disobedience would be "transgressing the very order of the cosmos".[1] Yet the "radical monotheism" of the Bible made such disobedience inevitable. Resistance to ruling oppressors—even active nonviolent resistance—was widely practiced, in the form of refusing to obey a decree, or by prophetically challenging a ruler's authority.

At the root of this resistance and active nonviolence was a deep sense of God's faithful covenant and reign; a sense that God does not approve of injustice, violence or oppression; indeed, that God abhors every ruling establishment which causes human suffering as it dares to take God's place. The Hebrew scriptures use two words to refer to the justice of God: *mishpat* and *sedegah*, often translated, respectively, as, "righteousness" and "justice." As James Walsh suggests in *The Mighty From Their Thrones*, to acknowledge the justice, the power, the *sedegah* of God, is to recognize that, in the end, God has the final say. God's word determines the way things are to be. God demands nothing less than total obedience to God and God's way of justice and peace.

Thus, the scriptures consistently prohibit idolatry in whatever form, and place all earthly powers, all temporal loyalties, all nation-states and empires under the absolute subordination of God. According to God's understanding of justice, we are told, God always takes the side of the poor, the outcast, and the marginalized. God always takes the side of the victim, and presses for justice and reconciliation from that viewpoint.

God chooses poor, powerless people, such as the shepherd boy David, to lead Israel and speak the truth for God. God even chooses the Hebrew people themselves, an oppressed tribe of slaves, to be what God calls, "God's own people." With the Exodus story, God demonstrates the will to liberate the oppressed—even if that means resisting and disobeying the imperial forces of death. God loves those whom the world accounts as nothing, and picks up their cause so that one day, all people—the oppressors and oppressed—will live in unity and harmony as the people of God.[2]

As Myers points out, there are generally two types of nonviolent resistance to evil that can be found in the Hebrew scriptures—whether performed by individuals, small communities, or large mobilized groups. First, there were acts of "defensive disobedience," aimed at protecting people from the violence and oppression of the ruling structures. This form of resistance primarily involved non-cooperation with laws and policies which oppressed people, legalized violence and upheld idolatry. A second type of biblical resistance could be called "offensive disobedience"—that is, direct action through confrontation and engagement, exposing moral, legal or political contradictions in existing rules and injustices.[3]

Moses' Mother

According to classicist and rabbinical scholar David Daube—in his book *Civil Disobedience in Antiquity*—the oldest instance of conscientious disobedience toward a ruling authority was the account of the birth of Moses, a story of 'defensive disobedience' (see Exodus 1:8-2:1).[4] When Pharaoh ordered that all Hebrew males be killed at birth, several Hebrew midwives defied Pharaoh's order, allowing the babies to live. Among those 'criminals' was Moses' mother, who hid the baby Moses; she thus knowingly and deliberately broke the law, for which she could have been killed. This tale of civil disobedience inaugurates the Exodus narrative itself.

Just as Rosa Parks' civil disobedience sparked the full blossoming of the civil rights movement, the civil disobedience of Moses' mother make possible the movement of liberation which followed: the Exodus event. Her refusal to submit to Pharaoh was a highly charged, political act of courage and resistance, and it is from such daring nonviolence that freedom can be born.

Indeed, one could say, her civil disobedience was the beginning of the end of Pharaoh's reign of terror. She was a serious threat to Pharaoh; her nonviolent resistance, like that of the other Hebrew women, helped crack open and bring down the walls of Pharaoh's imperial domination.

It is significant that, later, in the Gospel of Matthew, Jesus is portrayed as the new Moses: the new liberator.

According to Matthew's birth narrative, King Herod orders his soldiers to kill every first born male. Just as with Moses, Jesus' mother and father (with the help of the 'wise men') resist Herod by taking the child underground to escape.

Perhaps the most striking feature in this early biblical account of civil disobedience is that it was begun by a woman, by a group of women in fact; the victims of patriarchy. The Bible's long record of nonviolent civil disobedience begins among oppressed women. Among the women resisters who emerge in these pages are Esther, Tamar, and Rahab, (mentioned in Joshua 2, Hebrews 11:31 and James 2:25). One story in the first book of Samuel tells how Michal (David's wife and Saul's daughter), defied her father's order and sided with David in a showdown that ensured David's survival (1 Sam. 19:11-18).[5] Her disobedience to the king was an act of nonviolent resistance.

Daube notes that similar portraits of nonviolent, resisting women are also found throughout ancient Greek literature. For example, Sophocles' play *Antigone* is the Greek prototype of civil disobedience; its protagonist, Antigone, is a woman. Her character may be one of the first figures of nonviolent civil disobedience in all literature. Although the king had outlawed the burial of traitors, Antigone buried her brother, who had been executed for betraying the kingdom. Antigone declared, at one point, that the king could not "override the immutable, unwritten laws of heaven".[6] Such is obedience to a higher, nobler law—the law of love, the rule of God.

Rizpah

In the second book of Samuel, we find a similar story of civil disobedience in the tale of Rizpah. She protested King David's law forbidding the burial of her sons, and her outcry caused the king to change his position (2 Sam. 21:10).

As the story goes, the Gibeonites had executed two men and then received permission from King David to let their bodies remain hanging as a sign of disgrace. Such criminals were never buried. The mother of the two dead men, Rizpah, staged a sit-in protest at this policy. She "took sackcloth and spread it upon the rock and sat from the beginning of the harvest until the rains dropped from heaven, and suffered neither the birds of the air to come upon them by day nor the beasts of the field by night."

Her public mourning defied the king and was a bold, political act. Although everyone expected the king to punish—perhaps kill—Rizpah, her mournful, nonviolent resistance pricked his conscience and he allowed the men to be buried.

Tobit

In a similar tale, Tobit committed civil disobedience by burying the bodies of those killed by King Sennacherib of Assyria, who had executed many Jews and thrown their bodies behind the city wall. When the king heard that Tobit had defied the law by burying the bodies, he ordered that Tobit also be executed. Tobit fled just as the king's soldiers arrived to capture him. Shortly thereafter, the king was murdered, and Tobit returned home on his own. (Tobit 1:16-2:1).

We are left to ponder the nonviolent resistance and 'defensive disobedience' of Tobit, who survives his persecutor. This account resembles the modern-day witness of resistance by the four North American churchwomen who ministered to the poor in El Salvador at the height of government persecution in 1980. These women repeatedly prayed over and buried the bodies they found by the side of the road. Notes from the death squads were often attached to the bodies warning that anyone who touched the bodies would suffer the same fate. In acts of nonviolent resistance, Jean Donovan, Ita Ford, Maura Clarke and Dorothy Kazel buried the victims of the Salvadoran government's US-backed death squads. Because such decency and compassion were illegal in El Salvador, they, too, soon became victims of the same violence.

Esther

The book of Esther recounts Esther's campaign of non-cooperation with ruling authority. Set in a Persian court, this historical novel was intended to be a guide for the struggling Jewish community. As Daube writes, the book of Esther contains "several instances of civil disobedience, and though in themselves they are not perhaps momentous, the work is a piece of political indoctrination, with a veritable program."

In the narrative of Esther, queen Vashti first defies her own husband, the king Ahasuerus; this sets events in motion leading to Esther becoming queen. Meanwhile, the Jewish leader Mordecai refuses to pay homage to Haman, one of the king's governors; resulting in a potential retaliatory *pogrom* against the entire Jewish community. Esther, however, manages to persuade the king to overturn the edict.

Ched Myers concludes that the book of Esther was a handbook for the persecuted Jewish diaspora in its deliberations on concrete strategies of resistance:

> The message of the story seems to be that Jews who find themselves in positions of access to power, like Esther, must act in solidarity with those who take positions of noncooperation on matters of principle, like Mordecai.[7]

Like other scripture stories, it highlights the sacred duties of fidelity to God, repentance, and support for those who refuse to cooperate with evil. Such a text encouraged what we would now call nonviolent civil disobedience.*

Unnamed family in Maccabees

One of the most dramatic accounts of disobedience to imperial law is the story of the torture and martyrdom of the mother and her seven sons in the second book of

---

* It is also worth noting that Esther begins to take risks after learning about the plight of her people.

Maccabees 7:1-42. The episode takes place during the brutal reign of Syrian king, Antiochus IV Epiphanes (who ruled from 175 to 163 BCE).* One by one, all seven brothers are brutally tortured and executed—which the writer recounts in some bloody detail—as their mother watches.

Each brother makes a bold declaration of obedience to God just before he dies. As the second brother is flayed alive and scalped, he declares, at the point of death: "You are depriving us of this present life, but the king of the world will raise us up to live again forever. It is for God's laws that we are dying" (7:9). The fifth brother exclaims, "Since you have power among men, mortal though you are, do what you please. But do not think that our nation is forsaken by God" (7:16).

All the while, the mother watches her sons die, and she prays: "It is the Creator of the universe who shapes each one's beginning. As God brings about the origin of everything, God, in God's mercy, will give you back both breath and life, because you now disregard yourselves for the sake of God's law" (7:23).

The king makes special promises to the last son, hoping that the youth will disobey God's laws and follow the king's law. But the boy proclaims: "What are you waiting for? I will not obey the king's command. I obey the command of the law given to our ancestors through Moses... Like my brothers, I offer up my body and my life for our ancestral laws, imploring God to show mercy soon to our nation,

---

* This tyrant also becomes the focus of the book of Daniel, as we shall see.

and by afflictions and blows, to make you confess that God alone is God" (7:30-37).

Finally, the mother is the last to die. This dramatic tale of resistance and martyrdom upholds the example of a people who were faithful to God and God's laws. Rather than disobey God's law, they refuse to obey the king, and risk the terrible consequences of torture and death. Among others, their story is reminiscent of the struggle of the Salvadoran people who risk torture and martyrdom in order to remain faithful to God and God's laws of justice and peace.

Stories of prophetic nonviolence and resistance

The Hebrew Bible contains a running stream of 'offensive disobedience' too: from the Exodus event itself (the story of a mass movement of public defiance to a ruler) to the many prophets who encouraged active dissent .

According to the Hebrew Scriptures, prophets were pushed and driven by God to proclaim God's message to the public. Daube writes that "whether ultimately a friend of the powers-that-be or a foe, the prophet is more profoundly conscious than anyone else of a mission imposed on him [or her]."

The prophets saw their mission as telling the truth about God, and God's desire for justice. They would tell it to the ruling authorities who were oppressing and killing the poor masses. Sometimes, they privately rebuked the king or ruler in order to reform the ruling policy. On other occasions, prophets spoke boldly and publicly their message of condemnation to bring down the ruling authority. In every case, the Word of God challenged the ruling authorities and their reign of violence on the poor. Their truth-telling was subversive: a form of nonviolent disobedience.

Balaam's Donkey

The story of Balaam and the talking donkey in the book of Numbers (22:21-41) offers one such parable of civil disobedience. It highlights the prophet's duty to confront the evils of the king's policies, and to accept whatever the consequences that such truth-telling might bring.

According to Numbers, a donkey took its "heathen owner," Balaam, to see a ruler named Balak, King of Moab. Balaam had been hired by the king to announce the beginning of a war with the Israelites, by publicly cursing the Israelites.

As they were proceeding down a road for the appointed proclamation, an angel suddenly appeared in front of them, blocking the roadway. Balaam could not see the angel, but the donkey could. It was clear to the donkey that the angel intended to kill Balaam to prevent him from meeting the king and starting the war. So, in order to protect Balaam, the donkey started to turn off the path.

This deviation infuriated Balaam, who tried to correct the animal's direction. Because the donkey disobeyed him, Balaam beat the animal mercilessly. After the third round of disobedience, the donkey "spoke up" and asked Balaam why he was beating him.

Just then, the angel appeared plainly to Balaam, and Balaam realized that the donkey had tried to save Balaam's life. He repented of his violence towards the animal and had a change of heart about the upcoming war.

The strange tale continues, for Balaam had been inspired. Instead of cursing the Israelites, he disobeyed the king and offered them a blessing. The king was furious at Balaam's disobedience, and called off the intended military attack. Both the donkey's disobedience, and Balaam's prophetic word—uttered in obedience to God—prevented a war. As the story concludes, the Israelites were saved and in the end, even the king found peace.

This fable offers two parallel stories of nonviolent disobedience in obedience to a higher divine command. In the end, both the Israelites and the Moabites are saved from the horrors of war because of this nonviolent civil disobedience. Daube submits that, long before the story of Socrates, this story of the donkey's disobedience is the earliest account of accepting the penalty for one's nonviolent civil disobedience. It stands as one of the earliest and most unusual parables of nonviolent civil disobedience in the prophetic tradition—indeed, in all of ancient literature.

Elijah, Micaiah, Ezekiel, Jeremiah

Other prophets stood up to rulers as well. Elijah fearlessly questioned King Ahab in the name of God concerning the king's wars. In response, Ahab began a fast of repentance (1 Kings 21 :17-29). Later, Elijah spoke boldly to King Ahaziah, despite military intimidation (2 Kings 1:1-8).

In a similar account, the court prophet, Micaiah, defied the otiose King Ahab in his prediction of an upcoming war (1 Kings 22). Micaiah was thrown in jail, because he first mocked the forecasts of the ruler's men and then discredited the king's legitimacy in a parable. Daube comments on a connection between these "prophets of doom" and nonviolent civil disobedience:

> The prophet of good fortune is welcome to the party in power. It is the prophet of doom who violates the dominant interests, and is apt to go beyond what the rulers can safely tolerate; the prophet of doom is also apt to refrain from violence, be it on the ground of morality [or] be it on that of material weakness. When we consider the extreme contempt and hostility shown by many ancient seers and prophets to the authorities, and often in critical situations, when the latter were involved in a life-and-death struggle, the amazing thing is not that the prophet of doom sometimes suffered, but that he so frequently got away with it.[8]

The prophet Ezekiel was called by God to be a "watchman" for the people, ready at every moment to announce the divine warning/advice, and always willing to pay the price for these pronouncements (Ez. 33:1-11). Ezekiel took great risks announcing God's truth, and set an example of tireless, divine obedience—and the risk of civil disobedience.

The book of Jeremiah also includes brave symbolic talk. The stories about the purchase of the linen girdle (Jer. 13) and the earthenware jar (Jer. 19) dramatize the religious and social apostasy of the people. More often than not, Jeremiah's political denouncements and actions landed him in jail (Jer. 20 & 32).

In chapters 27 and 28, we read how Jeremiah symbolically protested the ruling authorities of his day by wearing a yoke around himself and calling upon the people to obey God, rather than become slaves to the ruling authority. Later, Jeremiah purchased a piece of land on the eve of the Babylonian siege of Jerusalem, to signal that hope lay not in futile violent resistance but in God's power to preserve the people through exile (Jer. 32).

In such ways, Jeremiah fulfilled the mission of truth-telling and resistance which God had given him, the power "over nations and over kingdoms, to root up and to tear down, to destroy and to demolish, to build and to plant" (Jer. 1:9-10).

"What is remarkable about 'civil disobedience' in the [Hebrew Scriptures]," Myers suggests, "is how Israel perceived its salvation story as so often contingent upon acts of non-cooperation with authority."[9] The prophetic word of the great prophets is nothing less than a call to do justice and make peace. It is a request that cannot help but challenge nations and empires which, by their very natures, do injustice and make war. If taken as seriously as they were meant to be taken, those outspoken declarations of truth would inevitably provoke a response from the ruling authorities, since they would be illegal. They demand a response; they provoke either conversion or punishment.

The word of God in these prophetic stories consistently proclaims that, ultimately, God does not support any particular national authority or political rule. God is the God of all people and all nations. Every person, nation and king is called to heed God's will and observe justice and peace. (See for example; Amos 1:2, 9:7; Is. 10:5-6, 19:24; Habakkuk 1:6). The prophets become entangled with the rulers of their times when those rulers cling to their power and refuse to obey God's will.*

Isaiah

The visionary, unsettling, yet consoling book of Isaiah begins with God's case against humanity, who have broken the covenant of justice and peace made with God. Like an aggrieved party, God makes God's case against the human race: "I no longer want your false worship. Instead, cease to do evil. Learn to do good. Search for justice. Help the oppressed. Be just to the orphan. Plead for the widow" (1:16-17). Jerusalem, the holy city, the symbol of the faithful realm, God declares, has become the home of "assassins" (1:21).

In contrast, through the prophet Isaiah, God offers a vision of peace and nonviolence: the mountain of God where all peoples will live in peace, where God reigns on

---

* And as Jesus would later remind his disciples, the prophets were frequently punished and killed for their words of peace.

earth just as God reigns in heaven. In that new creation, "God will wield authority over the nations and adjudicate between peoples; they will hammer their swords into plowshares, their spears into sickles. Nation will not lift sword against nation; and there will be no more training for war" (2:4-5).

The word of God proclaimed by Isaiah affirms the practice of justice. The one who does justice for the poor, who serves the needy and liberates the oppressed, we are told, is God's servant, God's faithful friend (Isa. 42:1).

Like the other prophets, Isaiah tells it like it is: God's people have been disobedient to God, but it is never too late to turn back to God (42:24). "This is the fasting that I wish," God announces through Isaiah. "Releasing those bound unjustly; untying the thongs of the yoke; setting free the oppressed; breaking every yoke; sharing your bread with the hungry; sheltering the oppressed and the homeless; clothing the naked when you see them, and not turning your back on your own... If you remove from your midst oppression, false accusation and malicious speech; if you bestow your bread on the hungry and satisfy the afflicted; then light shall rise for you in the darkness" (58:6-7, 9-10).

As in the book of Isaiah, the word of God—proclaimed from Hosea and Amos to Micah and Jonah—denounces the injustices and violence of the nations, and calls people to live peaceably and justly with each other in devotion to the one, true God.

In a world where injustice and war are legal, obeying God's call to make peace and do justice will always require, at some point, the illegal word and deed of God's truth to be expressed. This command of God creates a nonviolent army that summons people to conversion and transformation. Such a prophetic word of truth—spoken in those days by the likes of Isaiah and Micah, and in our own times by Martin Luther King Jr. and Oscar Romero—cannot help but shake the foundations of nations and empires, pharaohs and presidents. Though the messengers may be persecuted, imprisoned, and even killed for challenging the authorities of their day, the illegal word of God lives on. It is no less challenging today.

The apocalyptic nonviolence of Daniel and his friends

Though the book of Daniel could be classified as a tale of 'defensive disobedience,' it is so remarkable a work—the only apocalyptic account in the Hebrew Bible—that it deserves special consideration. Daube describes the book of Daniel "as a veritable charter of civil disobedience by a religious minority."[10] Indeed, it is one of the most revolutionary works of ancient literature, and next to the Gospels, one of the strongest manifestos ever written on nonviolent resistance and loving disobedience to ruling authorities.

Daniel Berrigan writes: "We have, in Daniel, a book about worldly power—and about the powerlessness of the believing community, revealed, ironically, as a new form of power... It is a story of providence, not success. A story of obedience and its risks."[11] The book of Daniel is, in short, a parable on nonviolence and the inevitable confrontation with the forces of violence.

The book of Daniel was written during the first half of the second century BCE, during the reign of Syrian king, Antiochus IV Epiphanes, just before the Maccabean revolt. Antiochus persecuted and tortured the Jews, as the story of the martyrdom of the mother and her seven sons reports. The unknown author of Daniel writes his story to inspire these persecuted people to nonviolent resistance and civil disobedience.

The controversy begins when Daniel and three Jewish friends refuse to eat unclean food served to them in the king's court. Such food violated their Jewish dietary laws (Dan. 1). Their disobedience progresses when the king orders an idol, a golden statue, to be worshipped. The punishment for refusing to worship the idol was death (Dan. 3). Daniel's three friends—Shadrach, Meshach, and Abednego—refuse to worship the image, and boldly tell the king:

> There is no need for us to defend ourselves before you
> in this matter. If our God, whom we serve, can save
> us from the white-hot furnace and from your hands,
> O King, then may God save us! But even if God will
> not, know, O King, that we will not serve your god or
> worship the golden statue which you set up. (Daniel
> 3:17-18)

The only concern of the three saints, as Berrigan points out, is their "unflinching faith and trust" in God. "Livid with utter rage," the king orders the three into a furnace. Later, the three are found "walking about in the flames, singing to God and blessing the Lord" (3:24). The fire, we are told, "in no way touched them or caused them pain or harm" (3:50). Thereupon, the king issued a decree honoring their God. "Trusting in God, [these three] disobeyed the orders of the king, and handed over their bodies, rather than serve or adore a god other than the true God," the king proclaims (3:28).

This parable highlights the biblical insight that those who trust in God, even to the point of death, will be protected by God. God will remain faithful to God's promise; our task is to be faithful to God, to God's way of nonviolence and justice. God saves them because they remain faithful, hopeful, and nonviolent. The high price of their civil disobedience is death; but in this case their nonviolence, their fidelity to God's will, is victorious.*

In the Gospels, this victorious outcome will transcend even death: Jesus will risk his life in obedience to God and civil disobedience. He will die, but God will raise him from the dead. In a sense, then, the book of Daniel portrays fidelity to God (via active, nonviolent disobedience to the ruling authorities) as an act of resurrection; a foreshadowing of the great revelation to come.

—

* It is worth noting that during the height of the civil rights movement, Martin Luther King Jr. cited this story in his *Letter from a Birmingham Jail* to defend his use of nonviolent civil disobedience.[12] King knew that though many African-Americans and their supporters would have to break unjust laws and risk their own lives, God would see them through to peace, as long as they remained faithful, steadfast, nonviolent, obedient to God and determined that God's justice be done.

As the story proceeds, the king announces that he will henceforth be recognized as a god, and that all his subjects must therefore address their prayers to him and no one else. Daniel refuses. He retreats to his room and prays 'illegally' to God.

Just then, the soldiers break in and find him praying. His divine obedience is rightly perceived as an act of civil disobedience. For this prayer, he is cast into the lions' den. As we all know, the lions spare Daniel. When the king arrives the following morning, Daniel is alive and well, forgiving and full of prayer (Dan. 6:22-23). This astonishing outcome causes the king to proclaim that Daniel's God must be acknowledged by one and all (Dan. 6:26-28).

Although the book of Daniel was written (or at least edited) in an epoch of violent persecution of the Jews and violent revolutionary activity by the Jews, it is significant that Daniel and his friends do not use any violence in their resistance. Daube points out that "the possibility of fighting does not occur to them; [it] is not so much as hinted at," despite the likelihood of death as a result of their disobedience:

> Indeed, in chapter two of Daniel, the hero saves not only the lives of himself and his three Jewish comrades but also those of the heathen wise men of Babylon. [In chapter five, notice] the sweet manner in which the Jewish heroes meet their antagonists; as the king comes to the lions' den into which Daniel was thrown the previous day, Daniel receives him with the words: 'Oh King live for ever!'[13]

The Book of Daniel is an apocalyptic work; indeed, one of the earliest known apocalyptic writings. But the key to all faith-based apocalyptic literature is steadfast resistance to oppression and idolatry through active nonviolence.

As the book of Revelation makes clear, apocalyptic writing urges patience and fidelity to the way of peace and love; it urges nonviolent civil disobedience towards the ruling authorities and their idolatrous violence. Such writing was intended to stir up the socio-political imagination of the oppressed, by renewing old symbols and re-appropriating Hebrew narratives of liberation; to envision a future in which God would restore justice and full humanity to all; and to demystify the pretensions and practices of the established order.

According to scripture scholar John Collins, the apocalyptic imagery in Daniel is a veritable political manifesto. It expresses the wisdom in expressing resistance not through violence, but through non-compliance, and endurance of what follows. It presents the reader with a very real battle, and a very real choice "between Michael and his angels, and the armies of Antiochus," where Daniel's apocalyptic visions of the future outcome must inform our decision.[14]

Daniel dreams of the "Human One" (Dan. 7:9-14) who will overthrow the rulers of the world, and transform their ways of violence through loving nonviolence. He thus inspires a revolutionary resistance of active nonviolence; and that inspiration makes possible the reality of a 'Human One' who *does* come. The community fosters the possibility.

Precisely when the "beast" of violence—the symbol of systemic injustice and imperial might—appears triumphant (7:3-8), a "counter-vision" is revealed. The beast is brought before a heavenly court and, along with the other nations, is judged and forced to relinquish its power to the Human One.

Myers suggests that the Gospel of Mark deliberately portrays Jesus as that 'Human One'—overcoming the violence of the worldly powers through the nonviolence of the cross—in order to inspire the disciples to a revolutionary (and consequently, illegal) nonviolence.[15] If this portrayal is true—and I believe it is—then the writer of the first Gospel deliberately saw Jesus in the context of the story of Daniel, a story of radical, illegal, nonviolent disobedience to worldly authority and steadfast obedience to God.

It is this profound example of revolutionary, illegal nonviolence that we must examine next: the life of Jesus of Nazareth. All the biblical seeds of nonviolent civil disobedience, from the story of Moses' birth to the prophetic words of Isaiah and the apocalypse of Daniel, come to fullness in the image of God as a nonviolent resister of evil, someone who willingly challenged legalized violence so that God's law of love and truth would be obeyed by one and all. The life of Jesus is the sacrament of civil disobedience.

THREE

The Revolution of Nonviolence is at Hand

Jesus and civil disobedience

Mohandas Gandhi, the great twentieth century apostle of nonviolence, once wrote that "Jesus was the most active resister known perhaps to history."[1] Jesus was a peacemaker who time and time again broke the laws that oppressed people and kept them slaves to injustice. Much that Jesus did was nonviolent, illegal, provocative, civilly disobedient and divinely obedient. Jesus was a nonviolent resister; indeed, a steadfast practitioner of nonviolent civil disobedience—a troublemaker *par excellence*.

To begin with, the Incarnation of God into human history is itself an act of civil disobedience. According to human law and imperial rules, God is not allowed to become human. God was supposed to stay God. God was supposed to remain in the image we humans created God to be: mean, violent, unjust, judgmental, imperial, warlike, awesome—like us.

If God were to be born into poverty, humility and suffering, into a life of active love and nonviolent resistance, it would be recognized by the powerful and elite as a judgment upon themselves (albeit the most sublime judgment ever). The birth of Jesus, the Anointed One of God—even in a humble stable, into terrible poverty, into the world of a family soon to become refugees, into an oppressed region of a vicious empire—is illegal.

In their attempt to justify their perspectives on the life of Jesus, the Gospel writers Matthew and Luke show how poorly received his coming among us was. The mother of Jesus, in the words of Luke, proclaimed that God "has scattered the proud in the imagination of their hearts. God has put down the mighty from their thrones and exalted those of low degree; God has filled the hungry with good things and the rich God has sent empty away" (Lk. 1:51-53).

In Matthew's account, King Herod was so enraged by the news of the birth of 'the Christ' that he ordered the murder of every male child under two years old, in the region of Bethlehem. The ruling authorities were trying to kill Jesus before he was even born! They realized that his power would challenge their own worldly power; like others, they mistakenly expected a militaristic messiah who would violently overthrow the systems of oppression and injustice.

Though Herod and his religious supporters misunderstood the nature of the messianic Jesus, who would wield the power of nonviolence and the power of powerlessness, they were right to expect a challenge from Jesus. The nonviolent Jesus would indeed set in motion the transformation of the world.

His entire life led up to the culminating confrontation with the powers of his day, symbolized in the oppressive cult of the Temple system. His civil disobedience in the Temple provoked the ruling authorities to arrest Jesus. They were afraid that his followers among the poor in the countryside would try to do likewise. So, he was imprisoned, tried, interrogated, tortured, and publicly executed by the ruling authorities. After his murder—through the legal channel of the death penalty—Jesus rose from the dead, another act in his series of nonviolent acts of civil disobedience to the imperial/religious authorities. His resurrection was nonviolent and illegal; indeed, totally outside of the law and its "principalities and powers."

Did Jesus know that he was heading for trouble? Didn't anyone advise him about the danger he was heading toward? Couldn't Jesus have stayed away from Jerusalem? Couldn't he have avoided those troublemaking encounters with the authorities? Why did Jesus make such a scene, such a decision? Why did he provoke such trouble? Why was Jesus civilly disobedient?

•

One of the critical points in Jesus' life, according to the Gospel of Luke, was the moment Jesus turned and began the journey to Jerusalem—where he would confront the Temple and all it represented, in the Spirit of love and truth (Luke 9:51).

The evangelists are clear on this point: Jesus was unambiguous. His disciples tried to talk him out of going to Jerusalem, but Jesus would hear none of that. He went to Jerusalem, fully conscious of the implications and consequences. He would speak the truth, dramatically, symbolically, at the center of the culture of death. He would turn over the tables of that culture, if necessary, but he would speak. He would insist on the truth. He would be obedient to God's will. He would make himself available to all.

He was willing to be rejected, willing to risk his life, but he would go and speak up for what was right. Jesus was a walking force of nonviolence. He was the living Spirit of the reign of nonviolence, walking amid the kingdom of violence. He lived the truth, and in his death, became Truth. His actions were the committed response of someone on fire with love and truth.

Thus, he was dramatic. He was symbolic. And he was willing to stand up to the principalities and powers and face every level of violence, including arrest, jail, trial, torture, and death by crucifixion. As a force of nonviolence, he would confront all these evils and overcome them through suffering love.

Two thousand years later, after millions of women and men have lived and died 'worshipping' the person Jesus as the Christ, 'the Anointed One of God,' the world continues its mad addiction to violence, rampant over-consumption in the global north and its continuing emission of lethal pollutants into the atmosphere.

In the nuclear age, suffering has taken on mass proportions not seen in earlier history. Millions of human beings starve to death while others, living in luxury, spend their energies on war and weapons of war, planning to inflict untold suffering on others. Warned by expert scientific opinion of an impending climate catastrophe, humanity continues to avoid taking the drastic measures required to protect God's creation from wholesale destruction.

In trying to respond to this challenge, few followers of Jesus dare to take the road to Jerusalem in their own lives. This is understandable: the consequences are still as severe as in Jesus' day—arrest, imprisonment, and, in some situations, torture and execution. Yet, following the leadership of Gandhi, Day, King and others during the twentieth century, a new strength has been given to Christians and truth-seekers regarding the road to Jerusalem, a way to re-read the Gospel through the eyes of nonviolence. What Jesus revealed was a Spirit committed to love and truth, and a way to live out that Spirit in a world of hostility and un-truth. Jesus' life, words and actions are the way of nonviolent resistance.

From this new perspective, this new hermeneutic re-learned from the court and the jail cell, the Gospel of Jesus reads as a manifesto of nonviolent civil disobedience to systemic violence and societal sin. It becomes clearer that the Gospel of Jesus commands active nonviolence. Everything in Jesus' life is seen as one illegal act of peacemaking after another.

Jesus was stubborn, insistent and determined: he would do everything he could, even if that meant going outside imperial and religious law, to reveal the reign of God. Once we understand the world as a reign of violence into which

God is bringing forth God's reign of nonviolence, Jesus' life becomes a testimony of nonviolent civil disobedience as a way to challenge the kingdom of violence and death.

Eleven episodes of civil disobedience

The Gospels portray Jesus as acting publicly to reveal the reign of God present in the world. They present a series of actions that build up to a crescendo in Jerusalem, where Jesus commits his greatest action: turning over the tables in the Temple, an act of peaceful, loving disobedience and truth-telling.

All his actions vary in focus and intensity; many are illegal and draw the ire of the ruling and religious authorities. But the three synoptic Gospels tell us it is the Temple action which leads to his arrest and execution. After his death, through the power of God, Jesus commits still another illegal act: he rises from the dead, and sets out inspiring people to the same series of subversive nonviolent acts.

His life is beyond our wildest dreams; but he says to us, "Believe it. Come, follow me as I turn over the tables of this culture of death." Jesus commands his followers to do as he did, to follow the spirit in the reign of nonviolence and its challenge to the kingdom of violence and oppression, even to the point of death, and then beyond, to resurrection. Let us examine, according to the synoptic Gospels, ten major episodes which I consider actions of nonviolent civil disobedience by Jesus, followed by an eleventh: the nonviolent act of resurrection.

1 — Proclaiming the words of Isaiah

I consider Jesus' proclamation of the coming of the reign of God in general, and his reading from the book of Isaiah in the local synagogue in particular, to be subversive acts of nonviolent civil disobedience.

The precise nature or character of his revolutionary subversion is simply the proclamation of the truth. Prophetic truth-telling in an imperial, violent society which oppresses the poor and marginalized is always civilly disobedient and risky. The truth is outlawed. Calling for justice and peace—not to mention a jubilee year—can only provoke arrest or assassination in such a state.

When Gandhi announced the start of massive, large-scale civil disobedience against British domination in India, he was arrested by the British—before he did any action. His words themselves were subversive and illegal. Jesus will eventually be charged with the same seditious activity: proclaiming to be a leader, the "king" of the Jews and stirring up the people with his ideas. I think that such truth-telling can thus be considered one form of nonviolent civil disobedience. Jesus started off this way, and he was in trouble from the start.

As the historian Josephus noted, Nazareth itself was the site of a small rebellion by a handful of people in the early part of the first century. In response to this subversion, the king ordered the crucifixion of two thousand men along the road leading out of Nazareth. It is important to remember that such a setting—a land of oppression and fear, a land of crucifixion—was the area where Jesus went public with his message of salvation and the coming reign of God.*

This region would have been markedly different from contemporary life in the West. It was the outskirts of the Roman empire; a state of constant terror and oppression; a territory of poor, farming people who were victimized by the Roman and Jewish leaders. Indeed, Galilee would resemble many of the war-torn countries of Central America or Africa today, where any semblance of activity on behalf of social change is considered revolutionary and subversive. In such places, one is grateful to have survived another day.

"The time is fulfilled, and the kingdom of God is at hand; repent, and believe in the gospel," Jesus declared (Mk. 1:15). Such words could not be anything but subversive within the context of Palestine in the Roman empire. Although Jesus' words went beyond the politics of this world into God's realm, the ruling authorities rightly recognized that their political authority was at stake. Jesus would have nothing to do with their violent, military rule; his God would reign, but through nonviolent love. Just as the prophetic proclamation of the truth by Oscar Romero and Ignacio Ellacuria in the violent world of El Salvador was a dangerous threat to

---

* Korean liberation theologian Ahn Byung Mu adds it is extremely telling that Jesus went to Galilee and began preaching the reign of God after John was arrested (Mark 1:14). Ahn maintains that Mark wanted to set Jesus within the political context of the spiritual, nonviolent revolution which John proclaimed, and for which he suffered and died. John the Baptist provides the political prologue; afterwards, Jesus took center stage, deliberately following in John's footsteps.

the authorities, so too, Jesus' proclamation was a serious challenge to the "principalities and powers".

Luke's account of Jesus' first public appearance in the synagogue at Nazareth describes an explosive scene. Jesus chose to read from the book of Isaiah, and deliberately picked the prophetic, political vision of a reign of justice. He "found the place where it was written: The Spirit of the Lord is upon me, because God has anointed me to preach good news to the poor. God has sent me to proclaim release to the captives and recovering of sight to the blind, to set at liberty those who are oppressed, to proclaim the acceptable year of the Lord."(Lk. 4:17-19)

"Today this scripture has been fulfilled in your hearing," he announced. This declaration was revolutionary: the announcement of the beginning of God's nonviolent revolution. To enact "a jubilee year," (as Isaiah refers, in the original translation, to Leviticus 25), would mean the complete upheaval of the entire class structure. The poor would receive justice; the entire economic system of land ownership would be reordered. His words *were* revolutionary. His listeners did not want to admit their faults, their need for repentance and conversion to justice; they were so enraged that they immediately tried to kill him. "And they rose up and put him out of the city, and led him to the brow of the hill on which their city was built, that they might throw him down headlong."

According to Luke, then, the proclamation of Isaiah's words were Jesus' first act of nonviolent civil disobedience. The same could be said of Mark's and Matthew's accounts of the proclamation of the reign of God. Like anyone who speaks the truth in places of oppression today, the truth-teller draws upon him/herself all the hostility of the unjust system. Jesus was lucky to have survived what may have been his first public words!

Joined by the disciples Simon, James and John, Jesus began teaching "as one who had authority." His first action was a public exorcism of a man with an unclean spirit in the Capernaum synagogue. This incident portrays Jesus disrupting the cultic atmosphere of the synagogue to reach out to someone in need of his compassion and love. The crowds are "amazed" at Jesus for his daring action.

This exorcism account explains the effect of Jesus' subversive proclamation upon his listeners. He exorcised the culture's possession of their lives and liberated them to a new way of life. The inner change and acceptance of Jesus' message meant that people would be "convulsed," turned inside-out. The unclean spirit of imperial violence, which had been internalized, came out of people with a loud cry (Mk. 1:23-26).

Nations and empires, by their powerful nature and evil spirit, seek to control every aspect of people—even their very souls. The liberation of people from the darkness of violence into the light of nonviolence (by, say, an active word of love and truth) could be considered a kind of spiritual civil disobedience. Jesus "cleansed" the person from the unclean spirit of violence and death which possessed him. The healed person now stood (with Jesus) in resistance to the culture.

Later, Jesus would "cleanse" the Temple. Both actions were amazing—and ultimately, illegal. From the personal to the societal level, Jesus would challenge the power of violence and death. For this first action itself, he was not arrested. He simply "arose and left the synagogue," we are told. But his provocative truth-telling and subversive exorcisms set the course for provocative confrontation.

2 — Healing the leper

A second action of civil disobedience was the healing of the leper. This act was civilly disobedient because it went beyond the designated boundaries of society, from those nebulous areas where some people are considered "insiders," to those clear-cut, off-limits places where others are declared "outsiders." In Jesus' day, lepers were "untouchables," a marginalized people cordoned off from society. One did not associate with lepers because they were believed to be "unclean" and cursed by God.

According to the synoptic Gospels, Jesus deliberately touched the leper who came begging to him, and in doing so, Jesus broke the sociological and religious barriers of society. He became a "leper" himself. Jesus was now a marginalized outsider: he had violated all the taboos. He too was now unclean.

Such a violation was civilly disobedient on a social level, but also broke specific religious laws of behavior. Gandhi's association with the "untouchable" caste of India exemplifies this scene. By renaming them as *harijans*, ("the children of God"), befriending them, living with them, and adopting their cause as his own, Gandhi challenged the entire cultural foundation of Hindu India, a challenge that alone could have provoked his arrest and death.

While many might have wanted to arrest Jesus for this subversive activity, and while some people may have been jailed and killed for doing precisely this kind of outreach to lepers, Jesus, again, was not arrested on this charge.

3 — Associating with outsiders

A third set of illegal actions would include Jesus' dinners with the marginalized, the outsiders of society. The Gospels make plain that Jesus regularly mingled with "sinners and tax collectors." He repeatedly associated with other 'outsiders' including prostitutes, the sick, the dying, the hungry, widows, women, fishermen, and children.

Aside from criminal offenders, the "sinners" referred to were those who violated the scriptural laws because they could not keep the standards of cleanliness, or because they were thought (by those in power) to have incurred the wrath of God. In many cases, the mere practicalities of their 'dishonorable' occupation made them a 'sinner': boatmen and shepherds because they could not rest on the Sabbath day; leather-makers or butchers because they had to handle things considered impure.

In other cases, people broke these religious laws simply by virtue of their poverty, or their sickness. As Ahn Byung Mu puts it, "these are not really criminals, but were forced into these situations because of outside pressures and religious social thinking. Religious sin and social alienation were really two sides of the same coin."[2]

As Catholic social teaching has it, Jesus took an active "preferential option for the poor and the marginalized," and this partiality got him into trouble repeatedly. In Mark 3:34, Jesus declared his total union with the poor and oppressed around him by announcing that they were "his mother and his sisters and brothers." Jesus saw himself as one with the outcast, marginalized poor.

In the story of Levi's call to discipleship (Mt. 9:9-13; Mk. 2:13-17; Lk. 5:27-32), Jesus dined with a social outcast. We are specifically told that Levi was "the tax collector." Then, we are told, Jesus "sat at table in his house" with "many tax collectors and sinners sitting" with him "for there were many who followed him" (Mk. 2:15).

Such behavior would have infuriated the righteous Pharisees and other authorities of the dominating class. By eating a meal with the marginalized, Jesus elevated them to the most sacred level of intimate relationship: as a brother or sister at table. Eating a meal with someone in the Jewish culture of ancient Palestine was a spiritual act. By sitting at table with a tax collector, sinners, and other public outcasts, Jesus must have shocked everyone. Jesus publicly embraced all those excluded by societal laws. His meal with Levi could also be considered, therefore, illegal, in its own right.

4 — Healing on the Sabbath

A fourth series of civilly disobedient actions could include all the public acts of working and healing that take place on the Sabbath. From the disciples' 'illegal' plucking of grain on the Sabbath (Mk. 2:23-28; Mt. 12:1-8; Lk. 6:1-5), to the healing of the man with the withered hand on the Sabbath (Mt. 12:9-14; Mk. 3:1-6; Lk. 6:6-11), to the healing of a woman on the Sabbath (Lk. 13:10-17), to the healing of the man with edema (Lk. 14:1-6), Jesus challenges the entire religious structure that oppresses the poor in the name of God.

According to Jewish law, the poor were legally allowed to glean from the fields. Jesus' disciples were caught plucking heads of grain on the Sabbath; their violation of the Sabbath law prohibiting all 'work' provoked offense. Jesus' followers were doing what was natural and they did it with Jesus' approval. They were hungry, so they ate the grain from the fields.

It is very significant, then, that the first public action of the disciples, according to Mark's Gospel, was to break the law (Mk. 2:23-24). The Pharisees, according to each synoptic account, were outraged that, contrary to the law, 'work' was being done on the Sabbath. They immediately asked: "Why are they doing what is not lawful on the Sabbath?"

Jesus responded with a reference to a biblical account of civil disobedience by none other than David himself—

eating bread from the Temple, "when he was in need and was hungry" (Mk. 2:25-26).*

Jesus defended their act of disobedience by citing the primacy of mercy in light of human need. "The Sabbath was made for people," Jesus asserts, subordinating Sabbath observance to human needs, "not people for the Sabbath." Such mercy is politically dangerous and illegal, for in the world of greed, power, and profit, there is no mercy. There are only rules, laws, and regulations to be blindly obeyed. Jesus' healing deeds turned over the tables of his oppressive religious culture.

This Sabbath episode exposes the hunger of the poor who cannot afford the luxury of observing a Sabbath law. Besides deflating the Pharisaic holiness code, the Gospel writers expose the politically revolutionary questions of land and food, as Myers writes:

> The disciples' commandeering grain against Sabbath regulations must from this perspective be seen as a protest of "civil disobedience" over the politics of food in Palestine. Jesus is not only defending discipleship practice against the alternative holiness code of Pharisaism, he is going on the offensive, challenging the ideological control and the manipulation of the redistributive economy by a minority whose elite status is only aggrandized.[3]

---

* Matthew adds another vital comment from Jesus: "If you had known what this means—'I desire mercy, and not sacrifice'—you would not have condemned the guiltless." (Mt. 12:5-7)

What is most significant about these Sabbath actions—in particular, the healing of the man with the withered hand—is their public nature, and the pointed questions which Jesus asks as he heals the poor. Jesus denounces the religious culture's inability to heal the poor and broken. By making others whole and by doing so publicly, Jesus reveals the corrupt nature of structured religion: its unwillingness to serve people, its complicity in keeping people ill, and the desire of God that all people be healed, that people treat each other with compassion and justice.

In each account of the healing of the man with the withered hand, for example, the Pharisees are waiting for Jesus to do something "unlawful" on the Sabbath, so that they might accuse him, and thus have him arrested and executed. Jesus directly, fearlessly speaks to their malicious plans. First, he notes that they themselves do good deeds on the Sabbath, like taking care of one of their animals; he exposes the inconsistencies and selfishness in their rules.

Next, he points out that helping another person is far more important than taking care of an animal. He asserts the dignity of every human being and the constant duty to be of service to other human beings. Then, he puts the question to them: "Is it lawful on the Sabbath to do good or to do harm, to save life or to kill?" When they refuse to answer, he heals the man publicly for all to see, and, according to each synoptic account, the Pharisees immediately plot to "destroy" Jesus. Jesus makes it abundantly clear that such issues are a matter of life and death, and he, for one, chooses to side with life. The Pharisees are quick to side with death.

Luke repeats the message with a story about the Sabbath healing of a woman who had suffered for eighteen years (Lk. 13:10-17). When the Pharisees challenge Jesus, he protests: "You hypocrites! Does not each of you on the Sabbath untie his ox or his ass from the manger, and lead it away to water it? And ought not this woman, a daughter of Abraham whom Satan bound for eighteen years, be loosed from this bond on the Sabbath day?"

Simply stated, "his adversaries were put to shame." His healing of a woman, and his naming her as a "Daughter of Abraham" were particularly compelling given the sexist structure of the society, where women were considered as sub-human possessions and slaves of men. Luke ups the ante a third time, by placing the account of a healing on the Sabbath in the home of a Pharisee, where Jesus heals the man. "Is it lawful to heal on the Sabbath, or not?" he asks. "Which of you, having a child or an ox that has fallen into a well, will not immediately pull him out on a Sabbath day?" Jesus' questions prick the pride of the religious authorities— and in this case, the lawyers as well, who are reduced to silence. Once again, they begin their sinister conspiracy to do away with Jesus.

5 — *Healing the Gerasene demoniac*

A fifth episode of civil disobedience addresses the economy of militarism, the business of war which allows the imperialistic forces of Rome to control people. The synoptics address Jesus' confrontation of Roman militarism, and its local support, in the parable of the healing of the

Gerasene demoniac (Mt. 8:28-34; Mk. 5:1-20; Lk. 8:26-39). Jesus entered the region of the Gerasenes where he met a man who lived among the tombs and was possessed by an unclean spirit. Jesus ordered the spirit to come out of the man. "What is your name?" Jesus asked the spirit. "My name is Legion; for we are many," the spirit in the man replied.

To the first readers of the Gospels, the term 'Legion' would have signalled an immediate reference to the Roman troops who occupied northern Palestine and kept the people in misery and under control. Since the Gospels would have been considered subversive literature at the time (as they are today in certain places), the evangelists, beginning with Mark, use this poetic language to make a political point. Jesus, we read, confronts the forces of Rome, and overcomes them.

As is usually the case, the local elite—who side with the oppressing empire and profit from its activities— fight to save the imperial forces. When the spirit begged to be allowed to enter a herd of 2,000 swine, Jesus gave it permission, and so it rushed down a hillside into the sea, where all the swine were drowned. Immediately, the local people asked Jesus to leave.

The thrust of the parable is simple: the price of healing the poor and thus healing society and the world from the forces of imperial death requires a total change in the status quo. The man possessed by the unclean spirit represents the poor of northern Palestine and elsewhere, who were under the oppressive and violent Roman military occupation. The herd would have been worth much money; the price of healing the man—the price of healing society—was extremely high.

It meant giving up their prize resource, the number one stock and money-maker: the herd. In order to be healed from Roman domination, people would have to let go of the profits of war and oppression; people would have to lose all the worldly benefits they had stolen from the poor so that everyone could be freed from their possession of violence.

The story is told to explain how challenging Jesus was—not only his denunciation of the oppressive regimes and imperial powers, but his call for the economic conversion from profits and oppression to justice and equity. Such a call would have been scandalous and radical, as indeed it is today—and no less fundamentally required.

The evangelists tell us that Jesus acted this way throughout his life. He confronted the imperial forces which oppressed the poor throughout Galilee and showed people how they could be liberated from oppression. The sad reality of this parable is that the Gerasenes chose not to accept Jesus' way of healing: they asked him to leave and never to return, saying in effect, "We don't want to be healed if it means changing our way of life, losing our business, making less money. We'd rather be possessed and live 'among the tombs'."

In our own times, such a message might challenge our silent acceptance of the nuclear weapons in our backyards, the profit that we gain from war, and the oppression that such militarism causes to the world's poor. It might challenge the unresolved legacy of slavery, which is still the origin of most modern Western wealth and inequality. It might challenge the global economy itself, where obscene profit for a dwindling few seemingly justifies the destruction of a liveable environment for most.

If we are to be liberated from violence, we will have to let go of our profits (much more these days than a herd of pigs), accept the healing which Jesus brings—and offer our resources to the poor, starving masses of the world. Today, for us to even approach God's reign of justice and peace, the entire world economy would have to be turned upside-down.

Jesus' message was not well received. The townspeople were filled with fear at his truthful word; the Roman soldiers and local ruling authorities wanted to stop Jesus from teaching his subversive message of revolution. As Jesus made the connections between militarism and economics, he practiced civil disobedience, as this parable explains. The authorities recognized the significance of his subversive teaching and direct action. They knew that if the masses of poor people in the outlying countryside accepted Jesus' call to nonviolent revolution, the empire would crumble. From their perspective, the only way to prevent such an uprising was to kill Jesus.

6 — Breaking the eating codes

Jesus also challenged the religious leaders of his day by breaking the legalized eating codes used to manipulate and oppress the Jewish people. According to Mark 7:1-23, Jesus' disciples did not wash their hands before eating. Mark stresses the point that, for the Pharisees and all Jews, one could not eat without washing one's hands. Such ritual practices were scrupulously upheld and watched by religious authorities.

Breaking these cultic observances—which were upheld in the name of God—would result in condemnation and ostracization. Few dared violate such religious laws. Jesus not only broke those laws, he called people back to the basics of justice and mercy, the original focus of the law.

When Jesus was questioned about his disciples' behavior, (Mt. 15:1-20; Mk. 7:8-13), he responded by questioning the Pharisees' infidelity to God's commandments: "Why do you transgress the commandment of God for the sake of your tradition? For the sake of your tradition, you have made void the word of God. You hypocrites!" Both Mark and Matthew quote Isaiah's critique: "This people honors me with their lips, but their heart is far from me; in vain do they worship me, teaching as doctrines the precepts of people" (Isaiah 29:13).

"You have a fine way of rejecting the commandment of God, in order to keep your tradition," Jesus declares in Mark 7:9. Matthew includes Mark's final explanation of the passage: "There is nothing outside a person which by going into that person can defile that person; but the things which come out of a person are what defile that person" (Mk.7:15).

Such words turned the whole of the Jewish law, as it was practiced, upside-down. They challenged the entire set of customs imposed by the Jewish authorities. These rules and practices, which required enforcement to work, enabled the religious authorities—the Pharisees and the Sadducees—to maintain control over the people. Such laws gave them a certain power and prestige, which in turn, led to economic profit. Jesus' words mark a 'religious' disobedience.

Today, an analogy can be found when women in the Roman Catholic Church celebrate Eucharist, much to the horror and shock of certain hierarchs. In being faithful, these women practice religious disobedience to the religious authorities in the church. They declare their obedience to God and civil disobedience to religious authority.

In chapter 11 of Luke, Jesus publicly rebukes the Pharisees and the lawyers for upholding pious practices while not practicing justice for the poor. While he was speaking, a Pharisee asked him to dine with him; so he went in and sat at table.

The Pharisee was astonished to see that he did not first wash before dinner. Jesus remarks: "Now you Pharisees cleanse the outside of the cup and of the dish, but inside you are full of extortion and wickedness. You fools! Did not the One who made the outside make the inside also? ...You tithe mint and rue and every herb, and neglect justice and the love of God" (Lk. 11:37-43).

Such strong language manifests the revolutionary mind of Jesus. He broke through all legalistic rituals performed in the name of God so that he could show us how far from God we had come, and how we could return to God. This 'good news' of truth threatened those who had long prospered and benefitted from misguided religious institutions.

Jesus' message was a plea for all of us to be human with one another, and thus to practice justice and mercy. *When we are just, merciful and compassionate, then God is pleased*, he insisted. *True religion is the practice of justice*, Jesus told the high priests and clerical aristocracy.

Such a message could only get him in trouble, for it upset the entire foundation of the religious culture of his time. It challenges the religious practice of our own time as well. The whole point of religion is justice and peace, he might say today; and yet, we are still very far from grasping and practicing this central truth.

7 — Loving the enemy

A seventh type of civil disobedience practiced by Jesus could be called his constant 'fraternizing with the enemy.' In a time of war or occupation, in a time of imperial domination, to associate with any enemy of the ruling authorities would have been illegal. Such behavior would be considered treasonous, as it is in any war, and could result in imprisonment and execution. Peacemaking, however, according to Jesus, requires not only associating with the enemies of one's nation, but loving them. Loving one's enemy during a time of war is dangerous, subversive activity—yet it is the hallmark of Jesus' teaching.

During the height of El Salvador's civil war, for example, it was illegal to associate with (or love) the enemies of the government—that is, to promote peace through dialogue with all sides in the war and asking all sides to stop the killing. Those who crossed boundaries to make peace and spoke with representatives of the violent right (the death squads, the government military forces, and the US military advisors) and the violent left (the revolutionary guerillas who killed Salvadoran soldiers) risked their lives. Each side, especially the domineering imperial power, was threatened by the dialogue.

Rutilio Grande and Ignacio Ellacuria were two Jesuit priests who associated with the poor and called for an end to injustice and war. Ellacuria, in particular, dedicated his life to ending the Salvadoran civil war by promoting a dialogue between all sides of the conflict. For his association with the revolutionary leaders (of the FMLN), he and his co-workers were assassinated.

His work was so illegal, so civilly disobedient, that they were not even arrested, tried or jailed. Associating with, and loving, the enemies of one's government threatens the profitable business of war—and its power of death over others. Thus, the martyred Jesuits and other martyred peacemakers were sentenced to death by some unknown military counsel.

Jesus practiced this same dangerous activity of illegal peacemaking. The Gospels are filled with references to the many times he crossed into 'enemy territory' and befriended the 'enemy'. Jesus associated with Samaritans, Gerasenes, and Greeks, to name a few such outsiders.

84

The Gospel writers take note whenever Jesus speaks with a Samaritan, such as the woman at the well (Jn. 4:4-43); not only because such people were considered ritually unclean, but because they were people from an enemy territory who waged war against the dominant order. The two perilous crossings of the Sea of Galilee in Mark's Gospel (4:35-41; 6:45-53) represent Jesus' reconciliation with 'the other side', the enemy territory; in this case, the land of the Gentiles.

From the flipside perspective of the Zealots, who hoped for a violent overthrow of the Roman occupation, Jesus' encounter with the centurion and the healing of his slave would have likewise caused trouble (Lk. 7:1-10). The centurion commanded one hundred soldiers in the service of Herod Antipas; he would have been considered the enemy of the people. Jesus' association with such a person would have infuriated the (violent) revolutionaries of his day.

Jesus preached and practiced the love of enemies. His actions enraged the religious and ruling authorities, who eventually saw to his execution.

8 — The entry into Jerusalem

Jesus's formal entry into Jerusalem could be considered an example of carefully choreographed street theater (as Myers has suggested); an impromptu, nonviolent, demonstration that undermined the authority of the empire. Jesus did not ask the crowd around him to pay him homage, to wave palm branches or sing "Hosanna!"—but he allowed them to do so (Lk. 19:39-40). As Myers notes, this procession symbolizes the coming of the humble, nonviolent messiah who will overcome the powers of death and empire in the world through suffering love.

Contrary to popular expectations for a warrior messiah, Jesus rides into Jerusalem on a donkey, the humblest of animals—and a biblical symbol of peace. As theologian Bill Kellermann writes, "Riding a donkey is a pre-eminently nonviolent posture, an act of humility, and a contemplative reminder of spirit and intent." [4] The crowds cry out, "Blessed is the One who comes in the name of the Lord".

Using scriptural images from Zechariah (9:9; 14:2-4), the evangelists prepare the reader for the nonviolent action at the Temple to follow. Yet, since much detail is given to the secret preparations for the procession into Jerusalem, the story must be recognized as making a striking symbolic statement in itself; thus, our eighth example of Jesus' participation in nonviolent civil disobedience.

Myers concludes that the procession is nothing less than a satire on the military parades of the empire. In a sense, Jesus is mocking Rome, and demonstrating how a real liberator acts: in humility, nonviolence, and simplicity. But the procession itself is public and political, like Gandhi's salt march to the sea, or Dr. King's march from Selma to Montgomery.

9 — Turning the Temple tables

The climax of Jesus' lifelong series of acts of civil disobedience is his nonviolent direct action at the Temple, the public center of the Jewish-Roman system.

The Temple system worked in conjunction with the Roman empire to keep the people subdued and oppressed. Jewish authorities held that God dwelt only in the Temple; it was there that the whole ideological order was anchored and legitimated.

To be faithful to God, one had to visit God in the Temple, and pay a considerable sum to the authorities in the process. Payment of the Temple tax was required. Roman coins, however, bore the emperor's image, and the emperor claimed to be God; since Jews were not to carry "graven images" of "foreign gods," the Jewish authorities developed their own Temple currency, exchanging Roman coins for their own money, and making a significant profit from the exchange.

Such a system pleased the Roman occupiers because it kept the religious leaders wealthy and happy, and kept the poor of the countryside preoccupied and at the service of the religious elite. The Temple functioned as a bank in itself; it was a source of loans, a depository for records of indebtedness. It was instrumental in an oppressive economic system which, through high taxes and interest rates, forced many a small farmer into indentured slavery.

"The high priesthood was so entangled with the Roman occupation," writes Bill Kellerman, "that it was all but a political patronage job, appointed by Pilate and subject to purchase and bribe... the Temple represents the intersection of the Roman money market and the local economy, the spiritual idolatry of status quo power."[5] Comparisons to our own time write themselves.

Passover, in particular, was the "commercial equivalent of the Christmas rush," as Bill Kellerman has it; a time when the population of Jerusalem would double, or even quadruple, in a city where religious tourism provided a key economic mainstay. Powerful interests were at work,

As Myers explains, for the Gospel writers, "the Temple state and its political economy represented the heart of what was wrong with the dominant system. [The evangelist Mark] had no wish for greater access to, or control over, the *cultus*—only its demise. In the same breath, [Mark] was at pains to reassure his Palestinian readers that God's existence was not tied to the Temple."[6] By turning the tables over in the Temple, Jesus symbolically turns over the tables of the whole culture and says, *"Enough of this imperial and religious domination. God demands peace, and justice towards the poor. That is how we are to worship God. True worship is the practice of faith and justice."*

Christians have justified every war, crusade and slaughter down through the centuries in the name of Jesus because they claim Jesus used violence on people in the Temple. But Jesus did not use violence. His whole message and action were staked on his claim of nonviolence. Jesus taught nonviolent love, even the radical, unconditional love of enemies; and at the heart of his teaching was a preference— accepting suffering oneself rather than inflicting suffering on others in the pursuit of justice and peace.

A careful reading of the text reveals that he hurt and killed no one; rather, he symbolically, dramatically criticized structural violence. He demanded that people convert, and the imperial system be abolished. The action in the Temple was nothing more—and nothing less—than an act of creative nonviolence. The killings of people in Vietnam, El Salvador, Grenada, Panama, Iraq or anywhere else cannot be justified by Jesus' action in the Temple; Jesus was nonviolently acting for an end to systemic violence and injustice.

Jesus nonviolently processed into Jerusalem, and then maintained a spirit of nonviolence as he entered the Temple. It is reported that he 'cased the joint,' as it were, and returned later the next day or so for his action. In effect, Jesus did a one-person sit-in; when he was not immediately arrested, he left. He made a bold, political statement; what Kellermann calls, "the most political [act] in all the Bible."

"Jesus is not engaged in civil disobedience in the classic sense of breaking an unjust law in order to change," Kellermann concludes. "He had often been taken to task for violating the Mosaic law, particularly around the Sabbath, but here he is not interested in improving the letter of the law, either Roman or Jewish, one jot. He is simply doing a strong action of visible truth in a place protected by law and authority."[7]

Ched Myers concludes in similar fashion: Jesus had come to Jerusalem to mount a nonviolent siege on the ruling class. His direct action at the Temple, Myers writes, is "the centerpiece in Mark's unrelenting criticism of the political economy of the Temple. Jesus attacks the Temple institutions because of the way they exploit the poor."[8]

Through Myers' eyes, the scenario resembles the nonviolent direct action that occurs regularly at military installations. Jesus "forbade anyone to carry any goods through the Temple" (Mk. 11:16). By sitting in a doorway or blocking an access road for an hour or so, one "shuts down" the place. But such actions are only temporary and symbolic, pointing to the day when the place will be closed permanently or transformed into a temple of peace.

Jesus' actions reached a climax at the Temple—the symbol of religious and imperial injustice which offended God and hurt the poor. The action in the Temple is specifically disruptive, going beyond the classic civil disobedience of Jesus' earlier episodes to militant, nonviolent direct action.

Following the action, he quotes Isaiah and Jeremiah, two prophetic voices who regularly condemned the Temple-state system. The whole Temple episode, then, is the fulfillment of the prophetic tradition's call for justice and peace.

10 — Resisting taxes

The episodes and teachings which follow the Temple action are a denouement of waiting, watching and explaining Jesus' nonviolence, as he awaits arrest and crucifixion. In these teachings, Jesus continues his nonviolent assault. In a series of parables and statements after the action, Jesus affirms that obedience to God is essential and that such obedience requires a similar faith and resistance.

Thus, Jesus encourages his followers not to pay taxes to Caesar, a declaration which was revolutionary and civilly disobedient (see Mk.12:13-17; Mt. 22:15-22: Lk 20:20-26). Later, during his trial, Jesus was explicitly charged with inciting people to refuse to pay taxes, an act of revolution punishable by death (Lk. 23:2).

The question had been initially put to Jesus by the Pharisees and Herodians "in order to catch Jesus" in the act of breaking the law: "Is it lawful to pay taxes to Caesar or not? Should we pay them, or should we not?" (Mk.12: 14).

Jesus recognized their hypocrisy, we are told, and asked, "Why put me to the test? Bring me a coin, and let me look at it." In each of the synoptics, these religious authorities reportedly produced a coin. In doing so, they would have been exposed by Jesus as hypocrites; as we have seen, religious people were not supposed to carry Roman coins, because every Roman coin declared Caesar to be god—an act of blasphemy in the mind of a faithful Jew. Besides revealing their hypocrisy, Jesus declared that God alone was to be obeyed. "Render to Caesar the things that are Caesar's, and to God the things that are God's," he announces.

If this declaration is consistent with Jesus' other words and actions throughout the Gospels, there can be only one interpretation: everything belongs to God, so everything must be rendered to God. As Dorothy Day put it, once we render to God what is God's, there is nothing left for Caesar.

In effect, Jesus told people not to pay taxes to Caesar, and then went beyond that to insist that everything one had was to be rendered (meaning handed over; submitted) to God. Jesus did not want anyone obeying the murderous policies of the imperial regime; he wanted people to enter the nonviolent reign of God.

Because Jesus had preached, lived and advocated voluntary poverty and radical obedience to God, he and his disciples had nothing to give to Caesar. If such practice caught on with the masses of people throughout Palestine, Caesar would no longer have the obedience of the masses. He would be out of power. When the rulers realized this political truth, coming just after Jesus' action in the Temple, Jesus was arrested and executed. They recognized the political nature of Jesus' divine obedience.

Unfortunately for us, his disciples down through the centuries have rarely practiced this teaching. Christians ultimately are called to live simply and not pay taxes (or specifically, money that contributes to injustice, the mass murder of warfare and the destruction of the planet) to empires or nations. They are citizens of the reign of God, for Jesus was a civilly disobedient tax resister.

After he turned over the tables of the money changers in the Temple and told his followers to "Render to God the things that are God's," Jesus had only a matter of hours before he was captured. But the Gospels confess his last urgent pleas to his disciples: to keep contemplative watch, to be on guard at all times, to love God and one another, to eat bread and drink wine in his memory, and to put down the sword.

He was tried briefly by the Roman and Jewish authorities, accused of "stirring up the people for a revolt, forbidding payment of the tribute to Caesar, and calling himself a king" (Lk. 23:2). He suffered the fate of all revolutionaries: brutal torture and execution. He died on a cross between two Zealots.

11 — Resurrection

Jesus remained faithful to God. His execution was a political event, as the trial accounts show. The forces of the empire brought the full brunt of their legalized violence down on Jesus. They used their ultimate weapon against him: he was put to death.

Yet, as the scripture recounts, the world had only just begun to see his weapon of nonviolence. God raised Jesus from the dead, and this resurrection was the ultimate act of nonviolent civil disobedience. God disobeyed the imperial code of law which says that the empire has the last word: when someone is executed, according to imperial logic, that person is supposed to stay dead. According to the logic of God—the logic of nonviolence—suffering love and truth-telling always lead to resurrection and life.

On the first day of the week, when Jesus' women friends went to anoint his body, they found the tomb empty. A young man, dressed in white, told them not to be afraid, but to get the others and go to Galilee where they would find him.

Jesus had risen and gone back immediately to Galilee, to the outskirts of the empire, into the land of the poor where he had started his nonviolent revolution. He was starting all over again! This time, his disciples would know the outcome: they would speak out publicly against the forces of oppression and injustice, risk arrest and death, and share in the resurrected life of the Christ.

The resurrection inspired the disciples to practice nonviolent civil disobedience towards the ruling authorities of the day, as a way of life. Shortly thereafter, the community of followers grew and multiplied and were martyred in large numbers by the imperial regimes. The resurrection gave them new life, hope, and the courage to continue resisting injustice and proclaiming justice for all.

The poetic story of Jesus' life, as told in the Gospel of John, ends with a resurrection episode of particular boldness. John's Gospel was written long after the others, perhaps seventy years after the death of Jesus. In the first account of Jesus' appearance to the disciples, Thomas was absent. When told that Jesus had appeared and offered them his peace, he laughed it off, saying, "I will never believe it without probing the nail-prints in his hands, without putting my finger in the nail-marks and my hand into his side."

A week later, Jesus appeared to the disciples—Thomas among them. Jesus said to Thomas, "Take your finger and examine my hands. Put your hand into my side. Do not persist in your unbelief, but believe!"

"My Lord and My God," Thomas declared as he fell in worship before Christ.

Thomas' response to the risen Jesus became the proclamation of the early church, the community of believers and resisters. But the words *'My Lord and My God'* were not just pious words uttered to Jesus in a prayer; they were political words of revolution. This creed, as a statement of belief, was an act of nonviolent civil disobedience.

A law had been passed declaring that the emperor was to be addressed from then on as *'My Lord and My God'*. Addressing Jesus with this title was not only an act of faith and an expression of love for Jesus: it was a highly illegal act. It broke the law. As far as the empire was concerned, it was an act of political blasphemy, because the emperor was god. The followers of Jesus who used this title, as John's Gospel hints, had taken up the way of nonviolent civil disobedience. They were no longer servants of the emperor; they had finally become followers of Jesus.

Today, we too are called to be a people who address Jesus—not the culture, the system, Wall Street or the state— as *our Lord and our God*. We are called to be people of the resurrection. As followers of Jesus, we take up where he left off: with the illegal work of nonviolent civil disobedience.

behaviors and letters, but the words filtered out as they were not helping; over is trying. At least it drove over they were pointed words or reveal. While reading a statement publishes a share of colors test and liketenant.

A key to all figure each decade realize that he needs he was to be understood from the rein at 16, 1920 and 25. Read As visible has visibility with kids and only able of rot faith and he was an out how he knows it is a uniquely utilized each ... into the turn the ... unite but other had in a small short political biography saved for any one's urged the ... these solutions you are ... that time is that any it mind ... where by the top of the basest ... there was there the letter one ... to be with ... that finite format faith ... and for ...

... make you ... have built it out for ... people who educ ... issue there of ... take a ... you want but like that decade comely ... fine the world ... need who are ... you by ... experienced ... feature in ... loan or ... the ... before he had ... up with had glad won't mood over ... it is ... moment ...

FOUR

We Must Obey God Rather than People

Stories of the early Christian communities

The Acts of the Apostles and other writings of the early Christians comprise a straightforward account of the activists who broke imperial and religious laws. Their illegal activity landed them in prison time and time again, until the authorities began executing them.

Today, such writings have frequently been dismissed by the institutional church and government leaders as quaint and archaic. Some suggest that these texts do not speak to the reality of life today. The early Christians may have been extremely devout and committed, it is said, but their actions have no bearing on life as it is lived in our contemporary world.

On the contrary, I want to argue that such documents have everything to say to us. When read through the political eyes of faith and nonviolence, they offer us a way out of our imperial predicament, our institutionalized violence, our apathy and civil obedience.[1] Indeed, the early Christians invite us anew to the faith which can move mountains, even in the face of nuclear empires and catastrophic climate change.

The book of Acts, in particular, makes more sense to me in the light of my own experience of nonviolent civil disobedience to institutionalized violence. Whenever I read the Acts of the Apostles these days, two occasions in my own life come to mind.

The first episode was a day of public witness at the US Military Academy in West Point, New York. One Fall day during the mid-1980s—as the US wars in Central America heated up—I joined a handful of friends, distributing leaflets calling upon the West Point cadets to refuse to participate in those US wars against the people of Guatemala, El Salvador, Honduras, Nicaragua and Panama.

As we walked into the common courtyard of the West Point dormitory complex, we were beseiged by hundreds of curious cadets who stuck their heads out of their windows to watch us distribute our message of peace. There was one catch to our Christian presence and invitation: we were on 'private property'. The police were called; we were arrested and whisked off in the back of a police car. Before we knew it, we were singing *Amazing Grace*—behind bars!

Our witness, we felt, fitted perfectly into the early record of the post-Pentecostal disciples who spoke out at the Temple in downtown Jerusalem. They, too, were hauled away for disturbing the peace.

Another occasion, on the anniversary of the bombing of Hiroshima, felt like a modern-day chapter of Acts. Some twenty-five of us staged a simple sit-in and prayer service at the entrance to a nuclear weapons and laserbeam warfare research center in downtown Manhattan. We were arrested, jailed and released for peacefully shutting down this center for the promotion of nuclear war.

Afterwards, a handful of us returned to the scene of the crime and sat down again. This time, the police put us through the system, carting us around town to various cellblocks. We were in and out of jails all day and all night. Finally, and unexpectedly, like Paul and Silas, at 6am the next morning, the door was opened, and we were released.

The early apostles were regularly in trouble with the law. Indeed, troublemaking seemed to be a prerequisite of the faith. Not only did the early Christians practice nonviolent civil disobedience; they were repeat offenders. Their commitment to Christ required public nonviolent witness; it required the giving of their very lives, as Jesus gave his. From the resurrection until the so-called conversion of Emperor Constantine, we note a deep faith in the early community that broke the laws of both the Roman empire and the religious authorities, a faith that cost the believers their freedom and their very lives.

Those lives became a loud *no* to the myth of empire, to the imperial liturgies and injustices which oppressed people everywhere. Instead, their witness sounded a new trumpet call: the good news of allegiance to the nonviolent Christ.

Acts of the apostles: civil disobedience

Almost immediately after the Pentecost event (Acts 2), the disciples were under arrest for speaking about Jesus, the name which had now been outlawed as criminal: the name of a state-executed revolutionary.

Upon healing a lame man, Peter and John spoke out publicly about Jesus to a large crowd, telling them to repent of their sins and complicity in the crimes which killed Jesus and continued to kill people. "As they were speaking to the people," it is reported, "the priests and the captain of the Temple and the Sadducees came upon them... they arrested them and put them in custody" (Acts 4:1-3).

When they were brought before the authorities, they declared that they had spoken out "in the name of Jesus Christ of Nazareth, whom you crucified, whom God raised from the dead." We are told that the authorities recognized them as associates of Jesus, and told them "not to speak or teach at all in the name of Jesus" (4:18).

Peter and John's answer set the tone for the public, nonviolent actions to come: "Whether it is right in the sight of God to listen to you rather than to God, you must judge; for we cannot but speak of what we have seen and heard" (4:19-20). They went on to denounce the ruling authorities for killing the Christ. Church historian Daniel Stevick writes that the disciples' basic message is quite simple, yet deeply revolutionary: "The nations and their rulers conspire against God and [the] Christ. The nations are God's unwilling servants. They are... a coalition of God's enemies."**2**

With that, the apostles took up the task of public preaching. For them, this was the twofold obligation of announcing the good news of Christ's liberation and justice, and denouncing the evils of injustice and violence. They began in Solomon's Portico at the Temple, until once again they were arrested and put into prison. On this occasion, an "angel of the Lord" opened the prison doors and told them to return to the Temple to speak (Acts 5:18-21). The apostles obliged.

They were arrested again, and brought before the council: "We strictly charged you not to teach in this name, yet here you have filled Jerusalem with your teaching, and you intend to bring this man's blood upon us," they were told (Acts 5:28).

Peter's response summed up the faith-based, nonviolent civil disobedience which followed, from those early days of Christian community through to today's nonviolent witness to Christ's peace and to His love for His creation: *"We must obey God rather than people"* (Acts 5:29-32).

The authorities had the apostles beaten, and ordered to stop; yet the apostles were not deterred, continuining day and night to violate the law which had been laid down before them (Acts 5:40-42).

They must have known what they were doing. Their illegal activity involved a risk they must have willingly, deliberately, even gladly undertaken. They hoped to convert everyone to 'The Way', the 'New Life' which they now knew in Christ. This new life of justice, nonviolence, community, and love rooted in faith offered liberation, forgiveness, transformation, and salvation to everyone (as they eventually agreed). Paying the price of their own freedom, even their own lives, was small in comparison to the good they hoped to offer to their fellow human beings.

Eventually, they did lose their lives for their continual nonviolent, direct action; but they always remained faithful, consistent and committed. In life, they shared in Jesus' way of the cross: a way of public confrontation with the imperial powers and religious authorities; a way of nonviolent civil disobedience and divine obedience. They knew, then, they would also share in his resurrection: the eternal life of God's beloved community; the reign of nonviolence, justice and truth.

•

The story which immediately follows Peter and John's testimony recounts the bold witness of Stephen, who preached about Jesus in very provocative, political language. He named those who were responsible for Jesus' death, and thus was stoned to death himself. He died praising God and forgiving his murderers.

Immediately after Stephen's assassination, the authorities began "a great persecution against the church in Jerusalem... Saul was ravaging the church, and entering house after house, he dragged off men and women and committed them to prison" (Acts 8:1-4). The disciples broke the imperial and religious laws, we are told, because their proclamations placed all authority and obedience in the Christ—not in Caesar, who was worshiped as a god. Their faith had been branded illegal by the authorities, yet the apostles and those first believers proclaimed Christ all the more.

Conflict was inevitable, yet their risky public witness continued. Acts 16 tells how Paul and Silas were arrested for breaking the law, and how they confessed to divine obedience, rather than civil obedience; they were dragged before the local leaders, attacked, beaten, and thrown into prison, their feet in the stocks.

Just one chapter later, a further story outlines the threats made against the early community. While Paul and Silas' teaching moved some of the Jews, "a great many of the devout Greeks, and not a few of the leading women" to join their movement, others from the Jewish community formed a crowd with the intent to cause Paul and Silas trouble. Unable to find them, they instead dragged Jason (who had accomodated them) in front of the city authorities, in their place (Acts 17:2-8).

Later in Corinth, the Jews and a proconsul named Gallio "made a united attack upon Paul and brought him before the tribunal, saying, 'This man is persuading people to worship God contrary to the law.'" As a representative of the early Christians, Paul was constantly accused of breaking the law with his talk about a 'new way of life', a life which called for the worship of God through active discipleship to the Christ, rather than the worship of the Roman emperor through the practice of war and oppression of the poor.

In Macedonia, Paul's teachings caused a riot; like Jesus' action in the Temple, Paul attacked the people's idolatry and false worship, in the hope that they would turn and worship the true God. In the confusion that followed, some prepared to bring charges against Paul and his friends— particularly, we are told, craftsmen whose wealth depended on making shrines of Artemis, worried that their trade would come into disrepute (Acts 19:21-27).

Later still, back in Jerusalem, Paul was attacked for his doctrine: "This is the man," his accusers said, "who is teaching everyone everywhere against the people and the law and this place; moreover he also brought Greeks into the Temple, and he has defiled this holy place." The people of the city seized Paul, and dragged him out of the Temple; the account is unambiguous: "they were trying to kill him". Ultimately, the tribune arrested him, and put him in chains (Acts 21:27-33).

In Caesarea, Paul was accused by Tertullus, "We have found this man a pestilent fellow, an agitator among all the Jews throughout the world, and a ringleader of the sect of the Nazarenes. He even tried to profane the Temple, but we seized him" (Acts 24:5-7). The trouble he caused eventually led him to face trial before Caesar, in Rome. Tradition holds that Paul was eventually executed by Nero.

A careful reading of The Acts of the Apostles, as Daniel Berrigan's book *Whereon to Stand* suggests, leads us to conclude that Paul was an active practitioner of nonviolent civil disobedience, a revolutionary for Christ. He paid the political price for his discipleship; and his leadership in the early community caused a public stir, marking the early Christians as troublemakers and rabble-rousers.

The call to civil disobedience in the New Testament letters

The letters of Paul

In the first letter to the Corinthians, Paul exhorts his friends to follow the wisdom of God in the crucified Christ, a wisdom which "none of the rulers of this age understand, for if they had, they would not have crucified the Lord of glory" (I Cor. 2:6-8).

In the second letter to the Corinthians, Paul's description of Christian life characterizes total obedience to God and Christ's way of life, an obedience that will inevitably have consequences in this imperial, violent world. Paul knew those consequences, and accepted them; he is quick to point out as much in 2 Cor. 6:4-10, listing the "afflications, hardships, calamaties, imprisonments, tumults, labors, watching [and] hunger" they endured.

For Paul, this obedience in Christ brought a radical freedom that transcended the law and all it symbolized. While Paul does not write within the apocalyptic tradition, he does invoke a spirit that rises above human laws. "Through the law, I have died to the law, that I might live to God," Paul wrote to the Galatians. "I have been crucified with Christ; it is no longer I who live, but Christ who lives in me." (Gal. 2:20-21).

The letter to the Philippians sets Paul in the context of prison. Paul is anxious to share the good news of the consequences of his proclamation of the gospel—how his imprisonment has led to the further proclamation of the Gospel of peace in Christ. "What has happened to me," he writes, "has really served to advance the gospel" (Phil. 1:12-14).

Paul proceeds to describe Christ's self-emptying life, death and resurrection, and how God "has highly exalted Christ [so that] every tongue [should] confess that Jesus Christ is Lord" (Phil. 2:9- 10). In doing so, he commits the civil disobedience that landed him into prison in the first place! He defies the edict of Caesar, who has proclaimed himself to be a god, "the Lord."

As he does elsewhere, Paul breaks the law in this very letter. "Our commonwealth is in heaven, and from it we await a Savior, the Lord Jesus Christ," Paul concludes in his letter to the Philippians (3:20). In his letter to the Colossians, he writes in the same vein, "God disarmed the principalities and powers and made a public example of them, triumphing over them in Christ" (2:15).

It might be incorrect to say that Paul was consciously breaking laws, as we might do today in the act of civil disobedience. Nevertheless, he was actively practicing a radical obedience to God in the risen Christ; an obedience that clashed with "the powers and principalities" of the day, i.e., the Roman empire and the religious authorities. His exhortations called the early communities to live according to Christ. They housed an unwritten assumption: that suffering, imprisonment, and execution would be the common lot of those who professed the illegal name of Christ.

Paul was a resister; his constant imprisonments and his martyrdom, though often neglected by the church and throughout the history of Christendom, require further reflection and study. The implications of his imprisonment and divine obedience call us to a deeper nonviolence, one that will inevitably bring even us to clash with our own imperial governments.

The letters of Peter

In this spirit, the first letter of Peter speaks of going to prison for the right reason. "Let none of you suffer as a murderer, or a thief, or a wrongdoer, or a mischief-maker; but if you suffer as a Christian, let you not be ashamed" (4:15-16).

Ched Myers notes that 1 Peter (and Romans 13) show a "genuine pastoral concern" about the motives behind acts of civil disobedience. The letters take a "firm stance against the excesses of offensive disobedience" and "pastorally encourage defined and controlled defensive actions":

> By the time the first letter to Timothy was written,, the "good fight of faith" is still conceived in terms of making a good defense before magistrates after the example of Jesus (1 Timothy 6:11-16). The writings of the time are full of concern about conduct in an era of persecution.[3]

As Daniel Stevick points out, "Such pleas reflect a time when, in the eyes and by the laws of the empire, to be a Christian at all was to be in a state of civil disobedience," with the very real possibility of suffering at the hands of the state. "The counsel of 1 Peter seems to be: Obey the state and live blamelessly, but you can expect to suffer for it."

The letter emphasizes "suffering for righteousness' sake" (3:14-15), suffering "for doing right" (3:17), reproach and suffering "as a Christian" (4:12-16), and suffering "according to God's will" (4:19). Stevick adds: "The early Christians praised the unyielding, steadfast, but gentle and Christlike way of meeting inevitable persecution."**4**

We should not be literal in assuming civil disobedience in the scriptures as it is understood today. Our motivations may be similar to our 'biblical cousins', as Ched Myers points out, but our setting is quite different. Even within the biblical accounts, we find a pluralism of approach, dependent on context. In court, Jesus remains silent, and Paul doubts the reliability of Roman justice (1 Cor. 6:1); but at other other times, Paul took advantage of the court setting to testify prophetically in front of the rulers of the day. This is a lesson in itself:

We should no more argue a reductionist position—*"no disobedience unless the Bible specifically stipulates it on a given issue"*—than we should a literalist one—*"every issue important to the biblical witnesses should be of equal importance to us"*... We must affirm the pluralism of the Bible in matters of civil disobedience style. The Scriptures are full of both offensive and defensive modes of confrontation.[5]

Nevertheless, "it is clear enough that civil disobedience in many forms is biblically justified and at times even imperative," Myers concludes. The failure of most Christians to acknowledge that is a problem of application, not translation. "For too long," Myers adds, "Christian teaching has been entrenched on the side of 'law and order'; perhaps there needs to be more theological attention given to the contemporary meaning of 'freedom from the law'."

Revelation: A manual for civil resisters

Myers calls the book of Revelation "a resistance document," a testament to the faithful who suffered persecution under the emperor Domitian in the last decade of the first century. "Chapter 13 is particularly recognizable as a call to non-cooperation with the Roman authority and an exhortation to Christians to accept the consequences of their resistance," Myers notes.

John, writing as a political prisoner in exile, objects to Rome, not only because of its persecution of Christians, but also because of its slave trade and oppressive economic structures (6:6; 18:3,9-20) and military policies (6:2-4,15; 16:13-21; 20:7-15). John insists that Christians must not only refuse to cooperate but also take steps to dissociate themselves from the imperial menace (18: 4-5).[6]

The conclusion of the book of Revelation describes the saints in heaven rejoicing and singing praises at the fall of Babylon, the Roman empire, and all such empires. All the prayers and the songs of the saints in heaven are prayers for the downfall of the empire. Such political prayers would be illegal in many places today for they criticize the forces of violence and death at work in the world. In the political vision of John of Patmos, we see a reign of nonviolence, the "nonviolent empire" of God—where "death shall be no more; neither shall there be mourning nor crying nor pain any more" (Rev. 21:3-4).

The book of Revelation, Stevick suggests, "is the most dramatic 'No' to the state in New Testament literature," in its description of illegitimate political authority. God, and God's people, are depicted in conflict with a tyrannous government making claims to absolute power—the 'beast', or rather, the Roman empire—with the dragon, Satan, shown as the true source of the beast's power. "The empire is set radically against God, but it does God the honor of mimicry," Stevick explains; the state calls people to worship itself, threatening death otherwise:

The state in this picture is arrogant, oppressive, universal... The imagery describes a malign, all-powerful, spiritual-political reality of which the early church – and many generations since – had intimate acquaintance.[7]

In short, the New Testament ends on a profound note of hope that the empires which wage war and break God's law will one day be totally overcome in the fullness of God's reign as proclaimed by the nonviolent Christ, the Lamb who was slaughtered and raised from the dead. Christians who follow in the steps of the Lamb of God—the illegal, revolutionary nonviolent Christ—will know the fullness of life in God's reign to come. Though they now suffer exile, imprisonment and death at the hands of the state, they shall one day share the resurrected life of a new world—a world free from oppression, empire and death.

Stories of early Christianity

Beyond the New Testament writings, the early Christians were committed to a way of nonviolent resistance. From the Christian way of peacemaking emerged the apocalyptic tradition—which consoles the persecuted, and calls them to resist all evil, no matter its earthly authority—a tradition which continued, "expressing the same clear but nonviolent opposition to Rome", through the writings of Irenaeus, Justin Martyr, Theophilus of Antioch, Clement of Alexandria, Tertullian, Hippolytus, Victorious—up to Lactantius in the fourth century. Church historian Ronald Musto explains all this, and continues:

The early church established itself from the start as an active opponent of pagan society. From the time of Paul, Christians identified themselves as a separate political people (Philem 3:20), a *polites*, a state, a kingdom, the true Israel, and, as Basil noted by stealing the very name of the empire, a new world community, the *oikumene*. The Christian movement aimed to liberate the victims of oppression, and thus had deep social and political potential.[8]

The empire, on the other hand, instituted "an imperial cult," which Musto explains, was "superimposed over and synthesized with local cults to form a standard of worship and political allegiance to the center." Worshipping the divinized emperor was not only a means of showing patriotism; it was a way for citizens to support the state, by imploring the aid of the gods.

> Every cult that aided citizens in supporting the state was a *religio licita* ['permitted religion']; every foreign religion following the ancient traditions of a conquered people that aided the imperial cause was a *religio externa* and thus *licita* for that people. Both were tolerated because they were both part of the life of an empire that was an all-inclusive religious, social, and political body.[9]

"By turning away both from the national religion of Judaism and the imperial cult of Rome, the Christians had neither gods nor political allegiance: they were, therefore, atheists and subversives," Musto writes. "Unlike the Gnostics, who were indifferent to the demands of the imperial religion, the Christians actively opposed it; the more the Christians became known, the more the pagan world reacted with fear and suspicion." Soon, the very act of celebrating the Eucharist was considered treasonous, and the public declaration of faith, that "Jesus Christ is Lord," was considered a capital offense.[10]

The earliest anti-Christian document is Pliny's "Letter to Trajan" written from Bithynia in C.E. 122:

> This is the course I have taken with those who
> are accused before me as Christians. I asked them
> whether they were Christians, and if they confessed,
> I asked them a second and a third time with threats
> of punishment. If they kept to it, I ordered them for
> execution; for I held no question that whatever it was
> that they admitted, in any case obstinacy and unbending
> perversity deserve to be punished. There were others of
> the like insanity.[11]

Christians were ordered to renounce Christ and worship Caesar by offering incense and wine to a statue of the emperor. "The issue appeared to the officials of the empire to be of [a] civic nature," Stevick explains. "One performed religious rites as gestures of patriotism or loyalty. Any superstition which produced obstinacy of the sort that some Christians demonstrated could be seditious in its tendencies."

"Pliny concluded that the Christian crime was the *nomen*, the 'name' or the fact of being a Christian, and not any *scelera* [or] individual crimes that Christians had committed." Musto adds. "For the Romans the very fact of Christianity evoked a set of attitudes that struck at the heart of the empire."[12]

One of the most moving testimonies of nonviolent resistance and an illegal allegiance to Christ came from Polycarp, an elderly bishop martyred in 156. His testimony was provocative and costly:

> The officer who arrested this venerable man tried to persuade him: "Why, what harm is there in saying 'Caesar is Lord,' and burning the incense, and so on, and saving yourself?" But Polycarp remained unyielding. He was brought to the arena where the crowd called, "Kill the atheists." The governor tried once again to dissuade Polycarp, urging, "Take the oath, and I will let you go; revile Christ," to which Polycarp replied, "For eighty-six years I have been his slave, and he has done me no wrong; how can I blaspheme my king who has saved me?" Moments later he was burned.[13]

In 165, the apologist Justin Martyr wrote:

> We who used to kill one another, do not make war on our enemies. We refuse to tell lies or deceive our inquisitors. We prefer to die acknowledging Christ. We who were filled with war and mutual slaughter, and all wickedness, have each and all of us throughout the earth changed our instruments of war; our swords into ploughshares; our spears into farming tools; and cultivate piety, justice, and love of humanity.[14]

In 178, the non-Christian Celsus commented on the refusal of Christians to participate in Rome's military campaigns or to justify killing. "If all [people] were to do the same as you, there would be nothing to prevent the king from being left in utter solitude and desertion," Celsus wrote.[15] He felt that Christians were,

> an illegal organization, were intolerant of and attacked the imperial cult, and therefore formed a revolutionary movement. They refused to defend the empire, they were arrogant and self-indulgent in their refusal to take on their duties as citizens. Their proselytizing destroyed the unity of families and homes, incited a rebellion that especially affected the poor and women and threatened the fabric of society.[16]

Both Tertullian and Origen wrote that some civil laws were unworthy of respect or obedience. Writing between 246-248 A.D., Origen writes that there are "laws that are not laws," and these are not morally binding:

> Where the law of nature, that is of God, enjoins precepts contradictory to the written laws, consider whether reason does not compel [a person] to dismiss the written code and the intention of the lawgivers from his mind, and to devote himself to the divine Lawgiver and to choose to live according to God's word, even if in doing this he must endure dangers and countless troubles and deaths and shame.[17]

Later, Origen continued:

We Christians no longer take up sword against nation,
nor do we learn to make war any more, having become
children of peace for the sake of Jesus who is our leader.
And no one fights better for the King than we do. We do
not indeed fight under him, although he require it, but
we fight on his behalf, forming a special army, an army
of piety, offering our prayers to God...

To those who ask us where we have come from, or
who is our commander, we say that we have come in
accordance with the counsels of Jesus, to cut down our
warlike and arrogant swords of dispute into plowshares,
and we convert into sickles the spears we formerly
used in fighting. For we no longer take sword against a
nation, nor do we learn any more to make war, having
become sons [and daughters] of peace for the sake of
Jesus, who is our Commander.[18]

"The legal charge always involved refusal to sacrifice
either to the emperor's image, as under Trajan, or to the
gods of Rome, as under Decius," Musto explains, "but the
real cause for bringing Christians to trial was the threat to
public safety that they posed." On September 13, 258, for
example, Cyprian of Carthage was charged with refusing to
make the imperial sacrifice. His charge read:

You have long lived an irreligious life, and have drawn
together a number of men bound by an unlawful
association, and professed yourself an open enemy to

the gods and the religion of Rome, and the pious, most sacred and august Emperors.[19]

Ultimately the source of conflict was the very nature of Christianity itself. It was illegal because "the early church was activist and sought to overturn the very fabric of Roman society," Musto concludes. "Conflict was inevitable. Rome recognized the danger and brought its power to bear, but it was not prepared for the Christian response," its nonviolent willingness to die for truth. Christians held their ground and were martyred by the thousands for their illegal, revolutionary faith.

"The ideal of nonviolence was early enshrined in the cult of the martyrs," Musto submits. Only by appreciating the blood of the martyrs can any discussion of Christian nonviolence proceed fruitfully. The nonviolent resistance offered by thousands of Christians to Roman society not only showed faithfulness to Christ's command to love one's enemies, it also achieved the fulfillment of the promise behind the command: after three centuries of persecution, nonviolence succeeded. Pagan society left the field exhausted, bewildered and defeated. The "story of the successful Christian revolution against the Roman Empire" thus was the single most important factor in the transformation of the Roman world.

In the middle half of the third century, Bishop Cyprian spoke out against war. "If murder is committed privately, it is a crime. But if it happens with state authority, courage is the name for it." An early church law from Egypt reads, "They shall not receive into the church one of the emperor's soldiers. If they have received him, he shall refuse to kill, if commanded to do so. If he does not refrain, he shall be rejected."[20]

In 291, the emperor Diocletian elevated the imperial cult to include the worship of his own person. He was attempting to revive the fortunes of the political empire by reviving the divinization of imperial power. Christians, Manicheans and other cults were among those to blame for Rome losing the protection of the gods; their refusal to participate in the rites of the Roman religion was essentially treasonous. Musto explains:

> Christians were to comply even if they had to be dragged to the altars and forced to go through the motions. In a religion of external act and formula this would have been enough to satisfy the gods. But to the Christian who believed in an inner spirituality the implications of the act went far beyond the question of loyalty; they evoked the conflict between Christ and Caesar, between the forces of compulsion and those of love.[21]

It was recorded that a Christian tore down the first edict of persecution posted by Diocletian. Another fearlessly seized the governor's hand in the act of sacrificing and exhorted him to abandon his error. Still another strode forward in open court and rebuked a judge for his ruthless sentences. When dragged to the altar and commanded to make a sacrifice upon it, one Christian woman even kicked it over.[22]

In 295, at the age of twenty-one, Maximillian was executed for refusing to fight for the emperor, essentially an act of conscientious objection, a form of civil disobedience. "I am not allowed to be a soldier," Maximillian said at this trial. "I am a Christian... I will not be a soldier. You can cut my head off, but I will not be a soldier of this world. I am a soldier of my God... My service is to my God. I cannot be a soldier for this world."

In 312 C.E., the whole tenure of faith and its consequences changed drastically when Emperor Constantine became a Christian on his deathbed. As Richard McSorley notes, "Constantine made it possible to become honorable in Caesar's eyes and also to be a Christian... This was a big change. With it the Christian attitude toward war shifted. No longer was the state the persecutor or the enemy. Now it was a friend, and soon it was a friend in need of Christian soldiers. The blessings that came to the persecuted ceased coming to many Christians. They yielded to Caesar's temptations and joined in Caesar's wars."[23]

As another scholar puts it, "With the accession of Constantine to power, the church as a whole gave up her anti-military leanings, abandoned all her pacifist scruples, and finally adopted the imperial point of view." Musto concludes:

> The early church was active in affirming Christian love, [and always] nonviolent in its means. Its activity was not restricted to an intellectual elite, but involved all levels of Christian life. Through the positive role given

to nonviolence, the Christian ethic aimed to overthrow Roman society by converting its heart and soul.

Thus the history of the early church demonstrates the principles of active peacemaking. It recounts a nonviolent revolution that attacked the roots of Roman social and ethical life by breaking down all the human relationships within it and setting them up again in a new way, mirroring the new relationship with God and humanity.[24]

The early Christians were, by and large, completely committed to the nonviolence of Christ and thus regularly civilly disobedient to imperial violence. However, with the emergence of Christendom, the light began to dim and their subversive faith subsided. Christians were now emperors, soldiers and warriors. Eventually, they would lead crusades, run extermination camps, torture their fellow Christians, and drop nuclear bombs on cities. Christianity strayed far from the peacemaking path of Christ.

A few shining examples illumined those dark ages, as Ronald Musto's masterly historical review, *The Catholic Peace Tradition*, makes clear. Such faithful witnesses as Francis and Clare of Assisi, Bridget of Sweden, Peter the Venerable (Abbot of Cluny), Benedict XII, John Colet, Thomas More, Desiderius Erasmus, and Bartolome de las Casas paved a road of evangelical witness for the great figures of more recent times. But what happened to the church, and what we need to do to return to that original fidelity, deserves further attention.

FIVE

Blessing the Empire

Seventeen hundred years of Christendom and civil obedience

Few Christians have risked the bold witness of declaring the peace which Christ insisted upon, which he offered as his resurrection gift to the world. Few have lived up to the invitation of Christ's life. Faithful remnant communities did survive through the centuries; but in the main, our Christian history has been a story of betrayal and accommodation to worldly power and worldly violence. The last seventeen hundred years has seen the story of an imperial, violent Christianity aptly named 'Christendom'.

In the twentieth century, infidelity and idolatry by Christians reached an apex. Under Hitler, Christians by the thousand went to church each Sunday, and looked the other way as Jews were slaughtered in concentration camps. Many Christians worked in those concentration camps, operating the gas chambers and ovens.

In South Africa, white Christians perpetuated the evil of apartheid against their black Christian brothers and sisters. In Lebanon, Rwanda, Bosnia-Herzegovina and Central America and now in Ukraine and Russia, Christians have waged war against one another, in the name of Christ, killing each other by the hundreds of thousands.

All over the world today, millions of Christians go to church each Sunday, and walk over the homeless on their way to work on Monday. Millions even work in munitions factories, or military or nuclear installations, in the fossil fuel industry or in the banks that fund it. Many work in various parts of the financial sector in the global north, promoting an unsustainable growth economy, responsible for making the poor increasingly poorer and the rich exponentially richer, day by day.*

How is it that we have strayed so far from the words and example of Jesus? How did we get where we are? Why has the expression of radical Christian witness been suppressed through the ages? And how can we stir up a new Christian fidelity?

•

The early Christians refused to kill others, manifesting a love for all and an illegal faith in God that led to their early deaths. Historian John Cadoux wrote: "Christians reserved to themselves the right of deliberately and avowedly disobeying the laws and orders of the state, whenever those laws and orders came into conflict with what they felt to be the law of God."[1]

---

* Pope Francis describes the global economy in this way: "The worship of the ancient golden calf (Ex 32:1-35) has returned in a new and ruthless guise in the idolatry of money and the dictatorship of an impersonal economy lacking a truly human purpose". (*Evangelii Gaudium* para 55).

As Roland Bainton wrote in his classic study, *Christian Attitudes Toward War and Peace*, "Prior to the advent of Christianity there is no record of anyone suffering death for refusal of military service."[2] The Christian community pioneered this nonviolent resistance. But with the empire's embrace of Christianity in 313 C.E., Christians in turn embraced the empire and all its institutionalized violence. Soon, Christians began to kill for the empire, renouncing the entire tradition of Christian nonviolence lived for three centuries in the early communities.

As one historian noted, Roman soldiers were now commanded to become Christians, and with this new religious fervor, "fought more ferociously and effectively" than ever. "Idealism, realized Constantine, is an exceedingly important element in military morale. The Constantinian bargain was simple and straightforward: the church received the protection and patronage of the emperor, and in return his military campaigns and designs were pronounced in advance to be part of the divine plan for the triumph of justice."[3]

Most Christians did not feel the need to turn their lives around, to take up the cross of nonviolent resistance to evil, to follow Christ. They could profess their faith in the comfort and security of the Roman empire or whatever war-making state of Christendom they lived in. Such misguided practices in the name of Christ led Gandhi to say, "I rebel against orthodox Christianity, as I am convinced that it has distorted the message of Jesus. He was an Asiatic whose message was delivered through many media, and when it had the backing of a Roman Emperor, it became an imperialist faith as it remains to this day."[4]

Christendom developed exactly the kind of religious structure that Jesus resisted. In his name, a system of false security and false worship was constructed which enabled those in power to hold onto the trappings (and traps) of empire. Few could resist the lure of 'security', greed and power which Christendom offered. Those who longed to live like Christ fled to the desert. They refused to compromise the Gospel, and most died unknown in poverty and in faithfulness to Christ.

But, by and large, the centuries of Christendom tell a tale of power and authoritarianism. The early Christian witness was abandoned in favor of structure, legalism, authority, and the 'holy' wars of the crusades. The classic collection of major church writings, Eric Jay's *The Church: Its Changing Image Through Twenty Centuries*, reveals an obsessive concern for papal supremacy. The church modeled itself on the empire it embraced, and created its own emperor (the pope) with its own regional procurators (cardinals, bishops and priests). Instead of Jesus' Sermon on the Mount, his witness of nonviolent resistance and his call to make peace, the ecclesial authorities established canons and rules to control the lives of believers.

The message of the Gospels was never quite lost. It was always there for people to examine. Unfortunately, for over 1,500 years, these texts were the sacred preserve of the monks and clerics who kept the Good News locked up, closed in books written in languages that few understood.

Indeed, the image of the Christ which emerged through those European centuries was that of an angry, violent man who counted every sin and waited with a vengeance to throw us all into hell.

We can point to many reasons for the misdirection of Christianity after those early centuries—the temptation to power, the lure of greed, the imperial ego, the trap of property, the cultural sin of injustice. One root cause was, and is, fear. The message of Jesus—a call to live life to the full by embracing all humanity in a risky love that does justice—is scary. Risking the life which Jesus lived fills us with fear. As Thomas Merton observed, the underlying cause of war is fear. As Scripture explains, the opposite of love is fear. Fear has plagued humanity since our creation. Jesus deliberately challenged our fears—especially our fear of death—by walking into Jerusalem, turning over the tables of our selfishness, and accepting the consequences.

When he asks us to follow him, he asks us to put aside our fears. As the western world developed over the centuries; as the rich got richer and the poor poorer; as wars of domination, oppression, extraction and acquisition were waged around the globe; people secured their souls in a fortress of fear. We are afraid to take Jesus seriously, to lose our lives, our possessions, and all that we have 'gained' in pursuit of his reign of justice.

We are afraid of truth, love, human variety and peace. We are afraid of God. We are afraid to suffer and to die for our part in Christ's redemption of humanity. Jesus speaks to these fears and insists that we put them aside, to walk with the living God in the Way of nonviolence. For many, his words are too much to bear: this was true fifteen centuries ago, and it is true today.

Once Christians became acceptable, and blessed the wars and injustices of the empire, they also began to settle down and acquire property. They no longer hid underground or lived constantly on the run, in fear of execution. Peter and John, according to Acts, had neither silver nor gold; but within a few centuries, Christian communities had acquired vast hordes of silver and gold—and land. Today, the Catholic Church is one of the largest land-holders in the world. While over half a million people are homeless in the United States alone, various dioceses and religious orders own enormous estates and institutions—acres upon acres of land. Such land ownership stands in sharp contrast to the poverty of Jesus.

In our history, few have preached, much less practiced, the message of voluntary poverty which is at the heart of Gospel peacemaking. Francis of Assisi and Dorothy Day stand out as two noble exemplars of this Christian mandate. Francis understood the Gospel truth of voluntary poverty. He saw that possessions lead to violence and war and are thus antithetical to Christ.

"If we want to own things, we must also have weapons," Francis wrote. "From this came all the quarrels and battles that make love impossible. And this is why we refuse to own anything."[5] Once Christians became landholders, they developed armies, guards, slaves and soldiers. Profits became the focus, rather than the truthtelling of Christian prophecy. It was not long before they declared a holy war to retrieve the Holy Land. They had indeed strayed far from the Gospel Way.

Dismantling the theology of compromise

A few texts in particular plot the path that the Christian community would take; signs of compromise can even be found in the writings of Paul. Though his writings and example are inspiring and heroic, they betray his blindness to certain Gospel truths. Paul was a victim of his age and culture, as we all are. Even as he wrote about the need to wage "spiritual warfare" against "the principalities and powers," Paul defended slavery and what we now call sexism.

Crucially, the passage of Romans 13:1-7 holds a great deal of blame for centuries of unconditional civil obedience to imperial and government whim. It is an extract that must be addressed if the call to Christian civil disobedience is to be taken seriously.

Paul's apparent bid to obey authorities

If Romans 13:1-7 seems like a call to civil subordination, it is essential to note its exact literary setting: within the climactic context of Paul's ethic of nonviolent love. Before the passage is Romans 12, a well-worn text highlighting the Christian duty of sacrificial love. It begins with "Do not be conformed to this world," continuing "associate with the poor; do not be conceited", and finally quoting Proverbs by saying "if your enemy is hungry, feed him" (Rom. 12:2-21).

After the passage concerned, Paul continues the theme by saying that "the one who loves his neighbour has fulfilled the law"; that the commandments are summed up in the sentence, "You shall love your neighbour as yourself" (Rom. 13:8-10).

The context for the exhortation of Romans 13:1-7, then, is Paul's clear, well-organized articulation of Christ's Way of nonviolence. Romans 12 spells out the implications for Christian faith to the Roman community. They are exhorted to offer their daily lives—in acts of charity, justice and peacemaking—as a sacrifice to God. This daily practice of the faith presents a new arena of worship compared to the older traditions: not the Temple, but the world, and life itself.[6]

Contrary to imperial wishes, many scholars have concluded that Paul does not advocate absolute and uncritical subordination to every authority. He encourages the Romans to recognize divinely sanctioned authority—but this is different, Donahue maintains, from encouraging them to recognize *all authority as divinely sanctioned.*

Obeying governing authorities outright would lead to a straightforward conflict with the ethic of Romans 12. One could hardly expect a continuity between the Christian imperative to overcome evil with good, and the methods of the Roman leviathan, which loomed over the Christians of the first century.

Paul instead exhorts occasional cooperation with a governing authority, on the condition it is "not a terror to good conduct" (Rom.13:3).[7] As theologian Charles McCarthy puts it, Christians must obey God first and foremost, and governing authorities only when they are in keeping with Christ's Way of nonviolence:

> What is meant is [that] you obey governing authorities to the extent that they act consistent with the will of God... Let us not be absurd. The statement is clear cut, and the statement is that when governing authorities say to do God's will, one does it when governing authorities say to. Anything else contrary to the will of God, one simply refuses.[8]

Paul never calls for blind obedience; he does not say, "Obey authority no matter what." The Greek word for obedience, *hypokouo*, does not occur in this passage. The imperative, "Be subject," *hypostassestho*, is a common expression in the New Testament. It occurs in the "household codes" (Col.3:18), in reference to Christ's victory (Phil.3:21), and in descriptions of slavery (Tit.2:9) and government (I Pet.2:18). Paul urges the Romans, *"be subject to authority; fit into society. Don't be a disruptive revolutionary force that will be more disruptive to the Christian community than it's worth."*

"The early church struggled to form an ethic of obedience and disobedience," Ched Myers writes, "because the [politically potent] nature of the kingdom seemed to radically contradict the atmosphere of imperial control in which the early Christians moved and lived."[9] Paul's admonition, "Let every person be subject to the governing authorities," (Rom. 13:1), implies that the *normal* Christian practice and response to the governing authorities required non-cooperation and nonviolent civil disobedience, in the tradition of the peacemaking Jesus.

Indeed, Paul struggled to articulate the meaning of this new-found freedom in Christ: a freedom and a lifestyle which transcended the imperial powers and principalities, but also required humility, to avoid gratuitous or exploitative conduct. He was trying to explain that faith in Christ does not *always* mean absolute *disobedience* to the empire or state; rather, that Christians could and should obey those authorities that do good, institute justice, and operate nonviolently.

Unfortunately, as Paul knew, such "authorities" were rare. Christians in Paul's time would always act under the presupposition that governing authorities did *not* recognize the authority of Christ. Myers adds that what was intended as an exception, a counterpoint to normal practice, too often became the complete, one-dimensional ethic of a church "no longer in collision, but rather in collusion, with the state."

The socio-historical context of this passage only reinforces the conclusion that Romans 13:1-7 is not Paul's treatise on government. Paul's audience, we must remember, is a minority people, without power, in a hostile world. The concept of a nonviolent democracy was unknown; people simply hoped to survive. The Christians Paul addressed had no part in state authority, and felt alienated and separate from it.

Paul is addressing a particular group of people, in Rome, probably around the year 58 CE. According to Tacitus' Annals, there had been a major tax revolt in Rome at this time. The Roman senate insisted on new taxes, even though the populace opposed the measure; the emperor Nero continued the taxes. Romans 13:6-7 is a call to pay these taxes; this is the concrete expression of "subjection" which is abstractly referred to in verse 1, where the command to "be subject" appears.[10]

Paul valued unity in the Christian community very highly. He pleaded with the early churches to stay united—and still be faithful. In this case, Paul was warning the Christians of Rome not to get caught up in the current tax revolt. He took the time to encourage payment of taxes because it threatened the unity of the fragile Christian community in Rome. Paul knew that problems and persecutions would arise, and so he concluded that this specific issue of taxation in Rome was not the issue to haggle over.

Jewish traditions, however, had one limit regarding the struggle to survive: the divinization of power. When governments claimed to be divine, they were to be resisted.[*] The law which demanded that the emperor be worshipped as a god would be the point at which Christians would stand

---

[*] We must remember, as well, that seven years after writing this, Paul was executed by the Roman imperial government because he resisted the divinization of civil power and insisted on the divinity (as well as the humanity) of Jesus of Nazareth.

up and be counted; and that day was, in fact, at hand. Paul wanted Christians to be united and prepared.[11]

Indeed, Paul clearly saw that the rulers of the world were set against God. Stevick comments that "the antagonism against God of the ruling forces of the old age is most clearly dramatized, St. Paul contends, in the crucifixion of Jesus."[12] The place where God was most clearly manifest in all history—the incarnation—was also where the organized structures of humanity showed their complete opposition to him. It is unlikely that Christ's followers would have forgotten so soon that it was under Caesar's authority that the Lord of glory was crucified; Christ and Caesar were set in such tension that Paul had to insist on Christians' proper subjection to state authority.

We cannot justly use a fragment of this letter to answer directly questions which arise out of other settings. From this passage alone, we do not know what St. Paul would have said a few years later when Domitian declared himself *"Lord and God"*, or two centuries later when Diocletian outlawed the church.

Still less do we know what he would say in a modern situation, in which a government had manifestly become an agent of terror to people seeking basic human rights. It seems certain that the apostle who began his ethical section with "Do not be conformed to this world" would resist having his comments in chapter 13 taken to mean unquestioning assent to the state. Paul, as a man in Christ, could never say, *"My government, right or wrong."*

Theologian-activist Jim Douglas observes in his ground breaking work, *The Nonviolent Cross: A Theology of Revolution Peace*: "Christ envisioned no Christendom, nor the possibility of there ever being 'Christian rulers,' except in the form of the satanic temptation which he rejected and overcame."[13] For Paul, the state is one of the "powers" of the world, overruled by Christ but still active. Moreover, the Christian could not expect the powers as such to abide by Christ's ethic. For the Christian to act as if the state's self-defined and self-protective ethic were in harmony with Christ's unbounded love—and could therefore be absorbed into his own commitment—would be an absurd contradiction.

The most important factor in Paul's mind was that Christians should be subject to the governing authorities just as Jesus was, no more and no less.* The Christian's responsibility was directly to the Christ of humanity, beaten and crucified; not to the particular state, which if it didn't always crucify Christ itself, could often as not be expected to leave him to die.

It is significant that many of Paul's letters were written from prison, and especially those letters written in Paul's name after his death (such as Colossians and Ephesians) were set in the context of his imprisonment. They stand as a constant reminder to the believing community of the cost

---

* When we remember that Jesus was executed by the governing authorities—a memory in the forefront of Paul's mind—this passage leads quickly to resistance.

of discipleship to Christ. Paul paid the penalty for his civilly disobedient faith; those who would also follow Christ, he maintained, must be willing to do the same.

In sum, Paul's advice is simple: Be subject to governing authorities as Christ was subject—nailed to the cross, paying the price for nonviolently resisting systemic injustice and oppression through civil disobedience and truth-telling. For Paul, Christ is our model in all things; we are to do as Christ would do. Such discipleship will result in crucifixion, or its modern day equivalent, for those who are faithful—as well as resurrection. Sooner or later, the authorities will demand total allegiance. On that day, we must be prepared to proclaim our discipleship to Christ.

Augustine: watering down the nonviolence of Jesus

Paul would have been astounded at any interpretation of his words which saw in them an ethical sanction for the state's conduct, and for the Christian's taking up the sword in its defense.

However, other authorities and figureheads within the church wholeheartedly encouraged greater compromise when it came to the nonviolence of Jesus. Augustine of Hippo is perhaps the most flagrant of these. Though he was eminently sincere (as the *Confessions* reveal), his words on war and peace did serious damage to the struggling community. In Merton's words, "Augustine is the father of all modern Christian thought on war."[14]

When Augustine pleaded with Boniface not to retire to the monastery, but to remain in the army and defend the North African cities from invading hordes, he set aside the teachings of Jesus for the teachings of the empire.

When Augustine wrote about peace having its root in order, he gave a subtle nod to the status quo of imperial power, and dismissed the prophetic witness and nonviolent resistance of the martyrs.

When Augustine wrote that war is sometimes an unavoidable necessity, that it can be just, and that violent defense is allowable, he encouraged and blessed the practice of war-making which ensued for centuries. He strayed far from the social teachings of Christ. His thoughts may have been civil, polite, and rational—but they were not Christian. Jesus taught, "Thou shalt not kill" and "Love your enemies." Augustine watered down that teaching, saying in essence: "Love your enemies, but if you cannot, go ahead and kill them."

Augustine believed that universal peace in practice was inconceivable. Thus, he wrote a lengthy explanation about how a Christian could kill, even wage war. "Love does not exclude wars of mercy waged by the good," he declared. It is possible "to love an enemy and still kill him," he maintained. In the fatal flaw of this lethal "logic," Augustine developed his "just" war theory and paved the way for centuries of warfare fought in Jesus' name.

"The history of the Middle Ages, of the Crusades, of the religious wars has taught us what strange consequences can flow from this noble principle," Merton concluded. Murder, war and even nuclear weapons have long been justified thanks to Augustine's theory of killing. The challenging nonviolence of the Gospel was quickly shelved so that the empire's wars of oppression could be blessed.

Augustine's statements clearly do not hold up in the light of biblical faith. They are contrary to the nonviolent Jesus of the Gospels. Augustine was mistaken, and the Christian community has paid dearly for his mistakes by quoting him in times of war and preparation for war. With Augustine, we betrayed Jesus and took up the sword.

The time has come to move away from Augustine's definition of peace as "order," and realize, as liberation theologian Miguez Bonino has stated, that such a theology merely justifies the status quo of the empire and its oppression against the poor and marginalized. The ultimate aim of the empire is not peace, but war; not democracy and justice for all, but benefits and privileges for the few who control the masses with fear and threats.

Aquinas: justifying war and murder

Thomas Aquinas took Augustine's reasoning to a new level of logic and efficiency. In the *Summa Theologiae*, Aquinas explained how both murder and war could be justified for Christians. Many have heard of Aquinas, but may not know that his reasons for permitting murder include the following:

If a man be dangerous and infectious to the community, on account of some sin, it is praiseworthy and advantageous that he be killed in order to safeguard the common good, since "a little leaven corrupteth the whole lump." (I Cor. 1:6)...

When the good incur no danger, but rather are protected and saved by the slaying of the wicked, then the latter may be lawfully put to death... Although it be evil in itself to kill a man so long as he preserve his dignity, yet it may be good to kill a man who has sinned, even as it is to kill a beast. For a bad man is worse than a beast, and is more harmful, as the Philosopher says.

It is lawful to kill an evildoer in so far as it is lawful in relation to the common good, which is corrupted by sin. The act of self-defense [which results in the slaying of the aggressor] since one's intention is to save one's own life, is not unlawful, seeing that it is natural to everything to keep itself in being, as far as possible.[15]

Aquinas relies on Aristotelian logic to reason his way to justified murder, and later to the justified mass murder of war. He bases his thinking on Aristotle, and so backs his positions with a reference to "the Philosopher" to justify his argument.

He should have relied on the Gospel spirit of nonviolent love as the groundwork for every ethical decision. Then his words would have been based on the teachings of the Christ. But he cannot, for Christ never justifies killing; indeed, Christ resists every form of killing. Like the disciples of the Gospels, Aquinas tries to find a way out of the nonviolent ethic of Jesus. Jesus, on the other hand, declares emphatically that there are no exceptions: his followers are to love so unconditionally, that retaliation, violent self-defense, violent resistance, and selfishness are unthinkable. We are to love even our enemies.

The Jesus of the Gospels presumes that such a nonviolent love is possible for human beings; if this nonviolent love and resistance were otherworldly and thus impossible, one concludes, he would not have been so insistent. Thus, we read in the Sermon on the Mount, that we are to be compassionate as God is compassionate, loving and kind even to the ungrateful and unjust, just as God is so loving and kind. Aquinas counters that such a love is not humanly possible, that our human nature demands violent self-defense, even mass murder in certain circumstances. His argument sets the tone for centuries of situation ethics, but it abandons the precepts of the Gospel, and thus can no longer be called Christian.

Aquinas fails to realize that we are all sinners, all of us are corrupt and capable of the most inconceivable evil. He has not understood God's nonviolence. The good news that he has also failed to grasp with his heart is the truth that every human being is a child of God, a brother and sister to us; that all life is sacred; and thus, that we cannot kill anyone, no matter how just and noble the cause.

Aquinas does not understand that the only way to promote and protect the common good—an end that the Gospel surely upholds—is through the way of goodness itself, through acts of justice and healing born from a spirit of nonviolent love. We are to overcome evil with good, Scripture insists. Yet Aquinas would do evil—he would commit murder for the good of humanity. Such unethical thinking had led to the torture and brutal murder of Jesus himself.

Caiaphas had used precisely Aquinas' argument when he argued that it was better that "one man should die for the people so that the whole nation should not perish" (John 11:50). For Aquinas, war is justified when waged for "the common good," when the cause is "just, when it is with "right intentions," and when the harm done by war does not exceed "the good" that comes from it. In reality, as Aquinas failed to grasp, such actions only further "the common evil".

In our own times, this logic of violence continues to be proclaimed as the Christian basis for war. In Vietnam during the 60's, the Pentagon announced, "We destroyed the village in order to save it." In Iraq, the Bush government massacred some 250,000 Iraqi people through a six week bombing raid which left a path of disease and destruction killing another 100,000 children alone in the weeks and months that followed. All this violence was committed in order to protect US oil supplies and send a signal to poor and dependent nations. Such atrocities, planned or carried out, are committed "for the common good" and "in the name of God." Such is the fruit of Christianity's embrace of the empire.

A distinctively Christian social ethic, I have come to believe, must always be rooted in the nonviolence of

Jesus. One cannot kill another person and still claim to love that person. One cannot wage war and claim to be a person of nonviolent love for all, a follower of Jesus. Aquinas, like Augustine before him, justified murder under certain conditions, even in the name of love, a love for the community. This is not the ethic of Jesus.

Thankfully, Christians are taking another look at the Jesus' ethic of *agape*, an ethic which precludes and insists on nonviolence at every level, and thus which rules out killing in each and every circumstance, including violence perpetrated against other non-human (or more than human) species, and against the planet itself. This consistent ethic of nonviolence, rooted in the nonviolent cross of Jesus, insists on an active resistance to injustice and a steadfast spirit of love. The Gospel insists that all the means towards the end of the good must be good themselves. It declares that, for the Christian, nonviolence is normative.

Jim Douglass thoroughly explored this precept of Christian discipleship in *The Nonviolent Cross.* "Suffering Love has the power to transform the oppressor, as it has already transformed the oppressed; it has the power to widen the community of strength," he wrote in his meditation on Christian nonviolence.

Douglass quotes Gandhi, who said that "Jesus lived and died in vain if he did not teach us to regulate the whole of life by the eternal Law of Love."[16] With nonviolence as the

---

* Also in his other works *Resistance and Contemplation, Lightning East to West,* and *The Nonviolent Coming of God.*

ground for all Christian conduct in the world, human life will be transformed, wars ended, and justice heralded as the framework for society.

But nonviolence is difficult to grasp, difficult to practice and difficult to explain. Douglass articulates "the logic of nonviolence" as a way of transforming relationships. It was this logic that Jesus followed, a logic which he upheld and offered to humanity; it is the logic of crucifixion, which will "lead the person of nonviolence into the heart of the suffering Christ". It widely differs from the philosophy of Augustine, Aquinas and Christendom.

People are able to commit acts of violence and injustice against others to the extent that they do not really see them as fully human, Douglass explains. The purpose of nonviolence, then, is "to move the oppressors to perceive as human beings those whom they are oppressing", to see the "humanity they have in common":

> The power of voluntary suffering [is that] the victim becomes no longer a victim but instead an active opponent in loving resistance to the person who has refused to recognize him as a human being... The suffering of his victim must be acknowledged by the oppressor as being human before he will cease inflicting it, and it is the love manifested in that suffering undergone openly and voluntarily which will bring him finally to this acknowledgment.[17]

For Douglass, "There can be no *ethical* justification even for the governing authorities bearing the sword, because the only valid ethic is that revealed by Christ in the Gospel, a love which does no wrong to a neighbor." Such love is nonviolent in each and every specific circumstance, including the cases raised by Aquinas. Like Augustine, Aquinas talked himself out of the Gospel, into a philosophical ethic and moral relativism which missed the point of Jesus' teaching and cross.

As Augustine and Aquinas justified the social sin of violence and mass murder in the name of the state, church authorities refined the new church laws which gave clerics and popes imperial powers. Centuries of theological reflection focused on these just wars and papal infallibilities, instead of on the simple compassion and active love which Jesus urged his followers to practice publicly in society.

It is essential that Christians today begin to reject Aquinas's rationale and embrace the irrational, illogical faith of the nonviolent cross, an ethic which prefers suffering for oneself rather than inflicting suffering on others as one pursues peace for the common good and nonviolent justice for the poor.

It is an ethic that demands maximum attention, faithful action, and total commitment. It is neither passive nor apathetic: it resists violence in every situation, but it does so through the truly reasonable approach of a love that does not hurt or kill others. In this spirit, transformation occurs and people are redeemed.

Most of us find this Gospel mandate difficult, but only because it is so rarely practiced in our own lives. We have so little experience of the Gospel in our lives that like

Augustine and Aquinas, we easily dismiss it as impractical, unrealistic or idealistic. The challenge before us is to put the Gospel into practice, to make it real today in our own bloody times. There is reason to hope: the start of a new history for the church is already being written.

A New History

In recent years, a whole parade of ordinary people have begun to take the lessons of Jesus seriously and put them into practice through nonviolent resistance to systemic evil. In the light of the world's wars; the stockpiles of nuclear weapons; the many thousands of people who die daily of starvation; the ongoing destruction of the planet's ecosystems and biodiversity—the time has come to accept responsibility for our systemic injustice, to correct our misguided theology and to put into practice the words of Jesus.

In September 2020, while the Coronavirus pandemic raged and the idea of 'returning to normality' filled public discourse, Francis reminded Christians of the opportunity and obligation to replace the reign of violence with nonviolence:

> Let us not go back to the "normality" sick with with injustice, inequality and environmental degradation. The normality to which we are called is that of the Kingdom of God, where there is bread for all and the social organisation is based on contributing, sharing and distributing.[1]

Like Martin Luther King Jr. and Dorothy Day, we must accept the active nonviolence and public resistance of Jesus as constitutive of the Gospel and act. A moral theologian once remarked to Daniel Berrigan that he spoke "about the Sermon on the Mount as though it were realizable now." His reply sums up the task at hand:

> An ethic of the interim, as I understand it, would allow us to fill the gap between today and tomorrow with the bodies of all who must die, before we accept the word of Christ. On the contrary, I think the Sermon on the Mount concerns us here and now, or concerns us never. In whatever modest and clumsy a way, we are called to honor the preference of Christ for suffering rather than inflicting suffering, for dying rather than killing; in that sense, all "interim ethics" have been cast aside. The time to obey is now.[2]

Such interim ethics have led us to the brink of nuclear holocaust, and is leading us now towards an irreversible climate catastrophe. A new way of thinking and acting is required *now* if the Gospel is to have any relevance for our lives. The events of the twentieth century, and the early part of the twenty first—from World War I, World War II, the dropping of the atomic bombs on Hiroshima and Nagasaki, the civil rights movement, the Vietnam war and the invasions of Iraq—have forced us to return to the Gospel and re-examine its meaning for our faith lives today. Nuclearism, imperialism, colonialism and human-induced environmental degradation call for a response from committed Christians. Such idolatries compel us either to nonviolent resistance or to acquiescence. There is no longer any middle ground.

When we look carefully between the lines of recorded history, and listen to the stories of the poor and the faithful, we find moments of resistance and nonviolence that in a saner world would not be held up as heroic, but simply, normal. The practice of nonviolence in active resistance to the powers of the state has a fascinating history.

Because history has generally been written as propaganda for the warmaking state, the history of nonviolent resistance breaks through only here and there, like the history of the poor and the oppressed. But there exists a history of nonviolent civil disobedience; our own modern times, in particular, have seen the blossoming of that history, even as the forces of evil flourish.* We may never know all of it, but we are beginning to scratch the surface of a deep undercurrent of human effort to transform the world.

Nonviolent civil disobedience has exploded in recent times in every variety of protest from illegal leafletings, pickets, marches and teach-ins to school strikes, boycotts, tax resistance, sit-ins, blockades, the hammering of nuclear weapons into 'plowshares of peace' to the ever-expanding inventiveness of environmental protests world wide.

———

* Several books record the creative and imaginative spirit of civil and religious resistance in modern history. See Gene Sharp's three-volume master piece, *The Politics of Nonviolent Action* (the most thorough examination of nonviolent resistance in modern history); William Robert Miller's *Nonviolence: A Christian Interpretation;* Howard Zinn's *A People's History of the United States* (an account of the history of the oppressed victims in that country).

We need to learn the lessons of this history, even as we try to create our own history, to fashion a world of peace from a world of war and a world of co-operation with nature rather than our ruthless domination of it.

•

Besides the historic breakthrough of St Francis' witness to nonviolence, the reformation gave a renewed interest in living the Gospel of peace. The Anabaptist, Mennonite, Brethren and Quaker traditions emerged from the reformation to offer a new alternative to Christian lifestyle, a way of living that rejected violence and returned to the roots of Scripture. After the reformation, civil disobedience (or 'Godly dissent' as it was called) was often used by persecuted church sects to affirm their right to the free exercise of the faith.

For example, during the 1650s, Quakers were not allowed to worship in Massachusetts; they were subject to heavy fines and banishment from the colony. According to a 1658 law, they could be executed if they returned. Many challenged that law, and were hanged; others were beaten, branded or had their ears mutilated.[3]

Throughout the nineteenth century, abolitionists who sought to outlaw slavery used nonviolent civil disobedience. Later, in the early part of the twentieth century, civil disobedience was adopted by women in an effort to win the right to vote in the United States and in Europe. Women were arrested and imprisoned by the hundreds, and by the end of that turbulent decade, they had won their struggle.

As Hitler and his program of racism and imperial domination rose to power, a group of German students who called themselves the White Rose resisted the Nazis by leafleting and organizing campus rallies against Hitler's policies.* They were subsequently executed; they gave their lives in the struggle of nonviolent resistance to Nazism, and their civil disobedient witness was a seed of liberation and peace.

The Norwegian Evangelical Church, a state church that included 97% of the population, was completely committed to resisting Nazism. Its bishops published a statement which declared: "God stands opposed to tyranny through the power of God's Word and God's Spirit. Woe to us if we do not obey God rather than humanity."[4]

After Roman Catholic Bishop Mangers publicly supported the statement, he was called in to meet with the Gestapo. When he was threatened and ordered to sign a document opposing church resistance, he replied, "You can take my head, but not my signature." Though Norway's nonviolent resistance did not completely hold off Nazi control, it saved the lives of thousands of Norwegians and serves as a model for non-military defense and civil resistance to foreign invasion. In the end, Hitler himself ordered his representative Vidkum Quisling to abandon his plan of forming a Nazi government in Norway.

---

* One of the most often asked questions of those who advocate nonviolent social change is, "How could you have used nonviolence against someone like Hitler?" As overused as this analogy might be, this question is significant, and often asked in a genuine spirit. It offers a teachable moment that too many of us have passed up.

In a similar fashion, the Danish government, under the leadership of King Christian, refused to cooperate with the Nazis' anti-Jewish legislation. Just prior to massive arrests by the Nazis, the Danish people systematically transported seven thousand Jews to neutral Sweden, saving their lives. The entire Jewish population of Denmark had been warned about Nazi persecution and ninety-three percent escaped. The organized nonviolent resistance caused Eichmann to declare later that "the action against the Jews of Denmark has been a failure."[5]

In Finland, organized nonviolent resistance to the Nazi takeover saved nearly two thousand Finnish Jews (only four were deported to concentration camps). When Heinrich Himmler, Hitler's chief of security police, demanded the deportation of Jews, the Finnish foreign minister told him: "Finland is a decent nation. We would rather perish together with the Jews. We will not surrender the Jews!"

After the Nazis invaded Bulgaria, Bishop Kiril announced that he would personally lead thousands of Bulgarians in a campaign of civil disobedience to stop the deportation and subsequent extermination of Bulgarian Jews. He would personally "lie down on the railroad tracks in front of the deportation trains," he told a Nazi commander. Meanwhile, Bulgarian churchworkers hid thousands of Jews. Many were accepted as 'converts' so that they would not be arrested (their conversions were considered only temporarily binding). In the end, through such nonviolent resistance, all of Bulgaria's Jewish citizens were saved from the Nazi death camps.[6]

In the mid-1950s, Dr. King and the civil rights movement explored the power of nonviolence in a public, peaceful, prayerful movement of civil disobedience to racial injustice. After the famous Montgomery bus boycott, King went on a month-long pilgrimage to India to learn more about Gandhi and his method of nonviolent resistance. When thousands of African-Americans throughout the country stood up to white racism, even to the point of imprisonment and death, it became clear that the black community had found a way to resist the laws which enforced racism and oppression. As Richard Taylor observed:

> King never claimed that nonviolent civil disobedience would cure all ills or bring in the reign of God. What he did claim was that it was a powerful force for uprooting the 300-year-old pattern of segregation that denied black people the vote, exposed them to vicious lynch mobs, confronted them day in and day out with humiliating signs reading "white only" and "colored," and denied them simple amenities like ordering a hamburger at a lunch stand. In a decade of nonviolent struggle, in which civil disobedience of segregation laws was a key tactic, the black movement totally shattered that centuries-old pattern that no other strategy had been able to touch.[7]

The nonviolence and civil disobedience of the civil rights movement sparked Christians and concerned people around the country to demonstrate during the 1960s and

1970s against the US war in Southeast Asia on a massive scale.

The witness of the Berrigans and the Catonsville Nine as they burned the files of a Maryland draft board center sparked the conscience of the church and the nation to speak out publicly, nonviolently and illegally, if necessary, to stop the US war machine in Vietnam and Cambodia. On May Day, 1971, thirteen thousand people were arrested for blocking traffic in Washington, DC. Though the war should never have been started, and went on far too long, this movement helped bring it to a halt and stayed Nixon's hand as he considered the use of nuclear weapons.

Since the 1960s, the movement of civil disobedience has dug deeper into the traditions and roots of nonviolence, but it still has a long way to go. Civil disobedience has been used as a tactic to oppose environmental destruction, the nuclear arms race, US intervention in Central America, support of the racist South African government, the death penalty, homelessness, sexism, inadequate health-care and the US war with Iraq. Out of this movement of nonviolence, a new community of resisters and believers is emerging. Indeed, as Christians take to the streets, a renewed Christian community is being born.

The most pressing demand before us now is to try to become faithful disciples of Christ, given the age we live in, and then to remain faithful, come what may. In this spirit, let us examine why the time has come for many of us to enact our faith through nonviolent civil disobedience to systemic injustice.

•

In 1986, on the feast of Pentecost, over 1,000 Christians from around the United States gathered for four days of prayer and reflection in Washington, DC.

We came from every denomination of Christian faith with a common concern for justice, peace, and the love which Christ missioned us to proclaim with our lives. The Sanctuary movement; Witness for Peace in Nicaragua; the Pledge of Resistance to US Intervention in Central America; the Overground Railroad; the Nuclear Train Campaign; the Free South Africa Movement; Plowshares activists, Catholic Workers, and countless others joined in "upper room" meditations.

Advocates for the poor, the hungry, the homeless, women, those on death row and more joined with peace activists from around the nation to read the signs of the times and search out a Christian response. After many hours of intense discussions and prayer, Timothy McDonald of the Southern Christian Leadership Conference told us that the time had come to "stop talking the talk and start walking the walk."[8]

We joined hands and processed from a downtown church to Lafayette Park across from the White House, where we sang and were missioned to proclaim the good news of Christ's peace.

Along the way, our procession twice knelt in silent prayer, that we might truly convey a Christian spirit of nonviolence and love. The joy, peace and tangible presence of the Spirit of the risen Christ moved us deeply. While we sang and took turns preaching the good news of reconciliation, those planning to commit nonviolent civil disobedience at various government headquarters came forward to receive stoles and a blessing for their mission of peacemaking. We broke into six large groups and processed out of the park to the various demonstration sites.

At the White House, Christians prayed and sat down on the sidewalk in a call for the abolition of war, nuclear weapons and the oppression of the poor. Over seventy Christians were arrested as the praying and singing continued. At the Supreme Court, protesters were arrested for calling for an end to the death penalty.

At the Soviet Embassy, demonstrators protested the Soviet war in Afghanistan and risked arrest. At the South African Embassy, activists refused to leave when ordered to disperse, and were arrested for calling for an end to apartheid. At the State Department, almost one hundred protesters sang, prayed and blocked the main driveway entrance, calling for an end to US warfare in Central America.

Altogether, 248 people were arrested that day in an effort to say publicly and prophetically the truth that US systemic violence must end, and justice and peace be practiced. That night, jail cells and holding blocks around the city quickly filled up with the singing and praying Christians. It was not long before the police began to ask those entering the jail if they preferred the "singing or non-singing section."

What a breakthrough in Christian witness! What a hopeful sign! A new church, a community of nonviolent resisters and peacemakers has been growing within the

United States! Yes, the systemic evils and injustices of the nation and the world are monstrous; but Christians in the United States on that day lived up to their calling by sitting down and standing up to declare a bold *NO* to death and war, and a joyful *YES* to life and peace.

It was a day to remember, a birthing moment, a *kairos* for the North American Christian community. For a moment, Christians in the United States came together in much the same way that Christians in those first Pentecostal days gathered in the streets, with the spirit of resurrection still fresh in the wind.

Civil Disobedience Field Guide

SIX

There Comes a Time to Cross the Line

Making the decision to disobey

For several years, my friends and I labored to stop US military intervention in El Salvador. Following the 1980 assassinations of Archbishop Romero and the four US churchwomen in El Salvador, we realized that the US government was financially and militarily supporting the Salvadoran government and their brutal death squads. These had systematically killed tens of thousands of campesinos, and US financial aid and military advisors had made it all possible. We listened to the stories of the suffering Salvadoran people, and began to put pressure on our government to cut all military aid to El Salvador and to stop all military intervention in Central America.

On several occasions, I was able to visit El Salvador, and for a short while in 1985, I worked in a church-run refugee camp in one of the many war zones. The faith and sacrificial love of the suffering people astounded me, opening my eyes to what a living Christianity could be. I was equally impressed with the many Jesuits who daily risked their lives in the nonviolent struggle for justice and peace for the Salvadoran poor.

On one particular trip to El Salvador, I was part of a delegation that journeyed to a remote, poverty-stricken village. Upon arrival, we discovered hundreds of soldiers, US military advisors and helicopters in the surrounding fields. The military officials, on this occasion, did not harass us, but the villagers asked us not to stay long, so we visited with them only a few minutes.

A group of women came forward and asked us if we would like to hold their babies. I reached out and took a child in my arms and felt my heart sink as I noticed its eyes glazing over, its bloated belly, the dirt and flies covering the infant. They were suffering from severe malnutrition and would likely die within days.

I looked up to see a squadron of machinegun-carrying soldiers, some thirty yards away, confiscating the community food supplies, including all its sacks of corn kernels. The military forces were literally stealing the food of the poor right before my eyes, in the presence of starving babies. It was a sight I will never forget, an image etched in my memory. The connection between war and oppression, violence and poverty, military might and the hunger experienced by so many in the developing world was clear. What I also noticed, written on the uniforms of the Salvadoran soldiers, were the words, "United States". This injustice was being committed in our names.

In the light of this experience, I could not help but speak out against a system which bombs and starves the poor of the world. At some point, it became clear to me that I had to cross over the line of civil obedience and legal observance to make public my extreme dissent. I knew I had to confront and resist the deadly system which kills the poor and threatens to destroy the human race, and to do so in a spirit of public, nonviolent love, with the hope that the people would be transformed and wake up.

I discovered that sooner or later, at some point, a time comes when we need to cross over the line of our liberal, legal protest, into that nonviolent, illegal, civil disobedience that risks our lives in the pursuit of peace and justice for the sake of the world's children, the suffering poor.

On the morning of November 16, 1989, I was busy at work in my community house in Berkeley when a brother Jesuit appeared at the door to tell me through his tears that six Salvadoran Jesuits and two of their co workers—people I had personally known and admired—had been brutally killed during the night. After our initial shock, we joined forces with friends throughout the San Francisco Bay Area and began to mobilize a public protest of prayer and civil disobedience. Our time had come. Together, we would cross the line, many for the first time.

Four days later, after an outdoor prayer service for peace at the Federal Building in downtown San Francisco, some 150 people of faith, including eighteen Jesuits, crossed the line onto federal property, knelt down and risked arrest in an illegal prayer for peace to the God of the Salvadoran martyrs. We prayed for an immediate end to all US military aid to El Salvador and Central America. That afternoon, we filled the jail cells with our hymns, and shared with each other the journey that had brought each one of us to that new moment across the line.

That day will live long in our memory, as will the countless other demonstrations for peace which took place across the country following the Jesuit assassinations. For many people, those days marked a new beginning; a new commitment to the Gospel of peace, a new solidarity with our suffering sisters and brothers of the world. Months of nonviolent civil disobedience followed in San Francisco, Los Angeles, New York, Seattle, Washington, DC, and elsewhere, until finally, US military aid was cut in half for the first time in a decade.

Though only half the aid was cut, and though it was quickly restored after a military offensive by the FMLN (the revolutionary front), the nonviolent, prayerful struggle, which included acts of civil disobedience, in a campaign for peace in El Salvador had made a positive difference. Our resistance helped give birth to peace in El Salvador. The witness of the martyrs, and the newfound strength discovered in active nonviolence, transformed our lives.

•

Civil disobedience is a way to express our dissent and outrage at the many government policies which do not promote life but inflict death on our fellow human beings. This form of active nonviolence—and the court appearances and jailings which follow—offer us, as people of faith, a way to risk our lives in a spirit of nonviolent love and steadfast obedience to the God of peace. We take this risk in the hope that the reign of God, a reign of compassion and justice, will one day be fully realized among us.

If civil disobedience is enacted in a spirit of nonviolence, prayer, community, and love; if it is carefully discerned to be God's will for us (as it was for Jesus and the early Christian martyrs); then it can be a great blessing, a modern translation of Jesus' way of the cross for our own lives.

Dorothy Day and Martin Luther King Jr. knew the power of this risky behaviour. They frequently went to jail for their public stand for the truth of peace with justice. They used the 'weapon' of nonviolent civil disobedience to wake the conscience of the nation. Dr. King was arrested on nineteen occasions during his short life to insist that the civil rights of all people be honoured everywhere. His witness helped promote positive social change, and perhaps more importantly, showed the world what it means to be a person committed to peace and justice; what it means to be a human being.

The decision to participate in civil disobedience

When civil disobedience is not enacted in a spirit of prayer and love, problems can arise. In such instances, it can easily become an outlet for the violence within us. A deep spirit of prayer and nonviolence must be maintained at all times and at all costs if our loving, civil disobedience is to spark a conversion in the hearts of other people.

We should not participate in civil disobedience if we are being forced into it by peer pressure, or by a compulsive need to assert our own egos, or by a need to exert our own power over others. Civil disobedience must be a free, humble, loving response offered in faith and prayer if it is to bear the fruit of peace.

We should be clear about our motives, and try to purify them whenever we are considering civil disobedience (even though our motives will never be entirely pure). Civil disobedience must not be performed for the purpose of gaining publicity on the evening news or in the morning papers. Something much deeper is at stake in an act of nonviolent civil disobedience.

Civil disobedience must not become a subtle expression of the violence in our own hearts. If it is an extension of our own warlike spirits, taken out on police or court officials, then it can serve only to inflame the spirit and system of violence which we oppose. Jim Douglass writes:

> Even in nonviolent resistance, unless we accept deeply the spirit of nonviolence, we can end up waging our own form of war and contributing to the conclusion we seek to overcome. Because the evil we resist is so great, we are inclined to overlook an illusion inherent in our own position, the will to transform others from the outside.[1]

Douglass warns of the "right deed for the wrong reason". Civil disobedience which empowers what Thomas Merton called the illusion of "the false self," is comparable to a personal act of war. It is a way of externalizing one's own frustrations into a form of theater, where innocence confronts evil. "But we are not innocent," Douglass adds:

> Civil disobedience in response to the greatest evil
> in history, done to empower a self which can't face
> its own emptiness, is the right deed for the wrong
> reason. Because of its motivation, it may also twist
> itself into the wrong deed. An ego-empowering act of
> civil disobedience will in the end empower both the
> self and the nuclear state, which while tactically at
> odds are spiritually in agreement. Such resistance, like
> the state itself, asserts power in order to cover a void.
> Civil disobedience, like war, can be used to mask the
> emptiness of a false self.[2]

In the spring of 1984, *Sojourners* magazine posed several questions for the Christian community to consider in its participative role in nonviolent civil disobedience. These questions challenge us to further reflection, and I repeat them here:

Does civil disobedience become our primary vocation [only] in a time of crisis, or is it rather undertaken in the midst of our many and diverse vocations and callings which continue to have integrity?

How can we be more self-critical of our own actions? What about the anger, hostility, and egoism that sometimes are hidden beneath the cloak of 'nonviolent' civil disobedience?

How really prayerful, humble, and joyful are we when we undertake civil disobedience?

In our sincere desire to call people to civil disobedience, are they sometimes being pressured or even manipulated into doing things they are not ready for or should not be doing?

What kind of pastoral process do we have to help people sort out their involvement in civil disobedience?

What new pastoral problems are created for those engaged in civil disobedience, especially where engagement leads to serious consequences and jail sentences?

What about the complicated and painful questions of civil disobedience and family responsibilities?

How do we put together civil disobedience with our other commitments to community and ministry?

What about the dangers of self-righteousness, bitterness, resentment, and judgment of others who don't choose civil disobedience?

How can we be single-minded in our commitments while at the same time respecting the integrity and diversity of Christian calling? [3]

Presenting these questions, Jim Wallis writes: "At Sojourners, we believe that nonviolent law-breaking can be a spiritual tool of rebirth and social change. However, we do not regard civil disobedience as the only thing, the most important thing, or the ultimate thing for faithful Christians to do." He concludes that *conscience* is what is needed, however it is exercised; that Christian conscience, Christian vocation, and the Holy Spirit's versatility must be embraced. "We hope and pray," he adds, "for a large movement of conscience in this country."

Wallis's questions require serious consideration if we are going to be true to the Spirit of peace and the love of God. They call us to the most essential ingredient in any act of nonviolent civil disobedience—a radical openness in our hearts to the loving Spirit of God.

If we are truly humble and loving, and if we walk in that Spirit of God's love, then we can rest assured in our divine obedience, trusting in the Spirit of God moving in us to bear good fruit. We can be free of judgmentalism, self-righteousness, egotism, bitterness or any violence in our hearts.

In conjunction with a disciplined spiritual life—searching to respond in-depth to God's love for all humanity—nonviolent civil disobedience can be a doorway into a deeper fidelity that touches many lives, and bears the good fruit of peace for generations to come. In this spirit, civil disobedience is not used to justify ourselves, or prove our commitment or assert our own domineering wills. Rather, it is a response to God's Spirit of love moving in us. It is offered as a gift given by God to us as a way to spread God's way of peace and love. When accepted and embraced, it can set forth a spiritual explosion of nonviolent love in other hearts which can transform our society and our world.

Jim Douglass suggests that nonviolent civil disobedience is a way to enact our prayer for peace, a way to risk publicly the prayer of Jesus, "Thy kingdom come, thy will be done." "Civil disobedience as prayer," he writes, "is not an assertion of self over against an illusion, but an acceptance of God's loving will because of our responsibility for evil: Not my will but thine be done. The prayer of the Gospels, like the prayer of Gandhi, is at its heart an acceptance of what we don't want: the acceptance of our suffering out of love. To be nonviolent means to accept suffering, out of love. The evil that causes suffering is an evil whose source is more deeply interior to ourselves than we have begun to understand. The prayer of civil disobedience which says, 'Not my will but thine be done'—by sending us to death or to that sign of death which is jail—is a recognition that in truth we belong there, and that we will in any event ultimately find ourselves there."

The most enduring things that can result from civil disobedience, as Douglass goes on to say, are the relationships formed to people who are touched by the act:

> The danger of seeing civil disobedience as an assertion of conscience over against the evil of the state is that it may get confused into an assertion against these particular people so that we may never really see our relationship to them as primary. Making friends with our opponents – in the police, in the Pentagon or in the Soviet Union – is our greatest hope of overcoming nuclear war.[4]

Civil disobedience rooted in love

Civil disobedience, in other words, must be rooted in love: the perfect love of God, a love which is nonviolent and forgiving towards everyone. In this spirit of love, civil disobedience can witness to the reign of God in our midst. Because of that spirit of suffering love, it can speed up the day when all people freely choose to do God's will.

As a community of peacemakers, the church is ultimately, I believe, a peace movement; likewise, the peace movement is ultimately much more than an effort to stop a war. It is a deepening of our spiritual roots as human beings, as sons and daughters of a loving, nonviolent God. As a people who can publicly articulate this spiritual reality that we are all united in God's love as sisters and brothers, inevitably, some of us, like Jesus, will be moved in the spirit of sacrificial love down the road of nonviolent civil disobedience to divine obedience.

When the United States began its massive bombardment of Iraq, many people across the nation took to the streets in peaceful protest. In other western countries, too, there were massive protests—a million people in the UK took to the streets in London to register their opposition to the British government's support.

Thousands of people committed civil disobedience in the United States by sitting in at the White House and at Federal Buildings in major cities around the country. In San Francisco, some ten thousand people marched in the streets each day during the first week of the war to demand an immediate end to the US bombing raids. The day after the US attack on Iraq, 1,087 people were arrested for sitting down in front of San Francisco's Federal Building. I joined that nonviolent protest and was arrested and jailed for the afternoon.

The next day, people of faith from around the Bay Area gathered for a prayer service on the steps of a church in downtown San Francisco and then led a funeral procession through the city to mourn and grieve over the outbreak of war, for the killing of people in the Persian Gulf.

As we walked to the Presidio, the West Coast Army headquarters, we knelt every fifteen minutes for a minute of silent prayer. At the entrance to the Presidio, we knelt again in prayer, and then climbed over a low wall onto government property where we knelt again in prayer. We were arrested, jailed and released later that day. The procession and action sent a strong signal that church people did not support the US war with Iraq in the Persian Gulf. We felt moved by the love of God at work in us to cross the line and say "No" to the war.

Such is the witness of nonviolent civil disobedience. It is one way of publicly, peacefully, prophetically addressing the world in the hope that the world will be transformed by God's love. As Christians, we have a responsibility to speak out like Jesus and say "No" to the deadly "principalities and powers" which inflict suffering on others, just as we are moved in the spirit to affirm life and peace.

We have a responsibility to call the world to the nobler principles of life and love. The Jesus we follow was civilly disobedient on many occasions. As disciples, we must at least ponder such a response for ourselves, as we seek to live faithfully in these violent times.

People of faith in particular need to enter this public search to respond to the wars and injustices which are tearing our world apart. Our role is not to become politicians; quite the contrary, we are called to witness, prophetically, like Jesus to the coming of God's reign of nonviolent love. This proclamation will require nonviolent protest, just as the early community was required to resist the empire and declare its allegiance to the Christ. Civil disobedience is a way for us as people of faith to enter this public struggle for peace with justice. Civil disobedience enables us to place our bodies on the line for peace, to be heard as human beings with a message of nonviolent love to all other human beings.

Such an act fulfills the very mission of the church itself: to proclaim the good news of peace, the Way of nonviolence, to the world. "The Christian always complains of the status quo, whatever that happens to be," theologian William Stringfellow once observed. The Christian "always seeks more than that which satisfies even the best ideals of other men and women. The Christian knows that no change, reform, or accomplishment of secular society can modify, threaten, or diminish the active reign of death in the world. Only Christ can do that," Stringfellow pointed out, "and now his reign is acknowledged." Civil disobedience is one way of actively, publicly acknowledging the reign of Christ over the reign of death. Stringfellow continued:

Christians do not believe in civil disobedience for its own sake, although they may resort to it from time to time as one of the tactics of witness vis a vis the nation. They engage in civil disobedience not in order to overthrow the rule of law and the authority of the nation, but to affirm the true vocation of the nation. They do so not merely as a means of changing public policy, but as a means of reminding the nation of its transience and ultimate impotence and of assuring it, even in the midst of its most grandiose pretensions to sovereignty over history, that only God is God.

But wherever the church and the Christians take recourse to civil disobedience, they willingly, readily, and freely bear whatever are the consequences of the disobedience. The Church, in that way, takes upon herself the nation's hostility toward God, accepts the condemnation of the nation, and is persecuted, suppressed, dispossessed.[5]

Humanity's disobedience to God and obedience to the idols of death need to be broken first and foremost by people of faith. If we are to live up to our calling to be peacemakers and ecological protectors, then we must at some point, on certain occasions, break free from the system which binds us and say clearly to the world that our obedience is with the God of peace and thus, that we oppose war and every form of oppression.

The problem of the world is its widespread obedience to the idols of death and disobedience to the God of peace. People too easily obey unjust, imperial authorities which threaten the human race, cause worldwide poverty, pursue the ruthless destruction of our fragile planet and inflict death on a massive scale.

Civil disobedience is a way to step outside the systems of death, a way to break free from the widespread civil obedience to systemic violence, so that the truth of our common humanity and the sacredness of life itself can be upheld for all to see. Plowshares activist Jerry Ebner says, "A willingness to accept imprisonment is simply the consequence of divine obedience. Subordinate is the hope that the act will help change the law and correct the injustice it protects by converting the hearts and minds of those who would maintain the status quo."[6] "Civil disobedience as prayer," Jim Douglass concludes, "is not an act of defiance but an act of obedience to a deeper, interior will within us and within the world which is capable of transforming the world."[7]

In *Divine Disobedience*, Francine du Plessix Gray describes Daniel Berrigan's response when asked why he burned draft files in the 1968 Catonsville Nine* action. It had not been a *useful* act, he explained. "How useful were the acts of the martyrs? How many martyrs ever had any practical programs for reforming society?" Since he and Phil Berrigan had started marching, picketing, lecturing and writing against the Vietnam war, the number of soldiers deployed had only escalated; they felt the peace movement had been on a plateau. Instead, the two had reached for an act

---

* See p.20-21.

"beyond politics: a religious act, a liturgical act, an act of witness." Destroying false idols, they believed, was a way to jolt people into justice:

> If only a small number of people could offer this kind of witness, it would purify the world. Wasn't there a time in England when every Quaker was in jail? What a great scene that must have been! Perhaps that's where all Christians should be today.[8]

Getting arrested, says Daniel Berrigan, is a sign that we "are not able to live with something intolerable."[9] Civil disobedience is a way to live in the truth of nonviolence, and to invite others into it too.

In the end, we commit nonviolent civil disobedience as a way for us to be faithful disciples to Jesus who carried his cross through Jerusalem and was executed for his nonviolent revolutionary peacemaking. It is a way for us to say with our bodies and our lives, "Let us live together in peace as God's children."

In 1971, the Catholic bishops declared that working for peace and justice is a "constitutive element" of our discipleship. Perhaps a day is coming when nonviolent resistance, including civil disobedience, will be a constitutive element of our discipleship. Some would say that day is upon us.

Civil disobedience is not absolutely necessary, nor is it our entire calling, nor the ultimate criterion for our discipleship. There is much more to our faith lives than risking arrest for peace and justice. Nevertheless, it may well be a significant ingredient for our life witness as we struggle to be faithful Christians. It is certainly an important addition and necessary consideration for all those engaged in the ministry of peacemaking.

In the times we live in—the *kairos* moment of starting to live, as we do, in the sixth mass extinction of the planet— the very claims of our identity as Christians are at stake. Discipleship with the nonviolent Christ may require the radical divine obedience which breaks the spirit of death that is enslaving the world. In other words, nonviolent civil disobedience may become a requirement for all of us as we pursue the narrow way of the Gospel in these dark times. In this way, when rooted in the Spirit of love, the prayer we take into the streets, by risky acts of nonviolent civil disobedience truly becomes sacramental.

search for peace and justice. Nevertheless, it may

████████████████████████████████████

████████████████████████████████████

With a few exceptions in the component of meaning to
analyze whether a full representation of the phenomenon
there is a great difficulty dealing as possibility as an attitude
identifying a while not infer. Given this, assume the
notion driving, behavior which need. The sense of deep
this developing forward in other people's attitudes. The
inadvertence a guidance for understanding one's respect
into the conscious of them, and in order to continue
do in, perhaps, ask in the rights of man the part of
being which has ... beaten the of note observ at,
absorbing nothing is with the ... consensus.

SEVEN

Preparing to Act

Following God's will to an action

A friend of mine, a woman in her sixties, found herself undergoing a dramatic change of mind and heart. For the first time in her life, she began to rethink our culture's attitude towards war and consumerism. She read the Scriptures from the perspective of the poor and wept at the implications.

After her conversion, she gave away most of her possessions and wrote a long letter to her children and grandchildren explaining her new primary concern for justice and peace. She travelled to El Salvador to see for herself the suffering caused by US militarism; she joined Christians in the Nevada desert to witness at the nuclear weapons test site.

After several months of discernment, she crossed the line onto the test site in an act of nonviolent civil disobedience to register her dissent from the nation's nuclear policies, and she was overcome with a deep sense of joy and peace.

That initial act of civil disobedience was, for her, a clear response to an urgent need to take a stand for justice and peace. She felt a keen desire to protest publicly the horrors of nuclear testing. In subsequent acts of civil disobedience in opposition to US military aid to El Salvador and the US war with Iraq, she began to feel a new Spirit within her, a deeper movement of the Spirit. She subsequently told me, "I no longer engage in nonviolent civil disobedience simply to promote justice and peace. Now it's a way for me to respond to the God of peace who is calling me to a new and deeper level of faith and obedience. I feel God calling me, moving in me, inviting me to act publicly and I want to respond to God. I want to be faithful to this God who calls me."

A discerning attitude and prayerful reflection are necessary ingredients in preparation for civil disobedience. Ultimately, an act of nonviolent civil disobedience is an act of divine obedience; that is, it is a response to the movement of God's spirit in our world, encouraging us to stand up and risk a public act of peacemaking on behalf of those who suffer.

It is a way to respond publicly, faithfully, and politically to our nonviolent God. Ideally, our engagement in civil disobedience should always come as a response to this movement of God in our lives. It should be a response to God's love, to God's spirit of peace inviting us to take another step in peace for peace.

Can civil disobedience be enacted in a spirit of unconditional love, forgiveness, and truth? Can civil disobedience be an act of prayer? Can civil disobedience be rooted in nonviolence down to the very core of our being? If it is discerned in a prayerful spirit and prepared for in a thoughtful, careful manner, it can. We do not engage in civil disobedience to tally the number of times we have been arrested for demonstrating, as in some modern kind of indulgence to earn our way into heaven.*

Nonviolent civil disobedience is not *the* one and only way to God, but *a* way to God, a way to witness to the peace of Christ in our violent world. It is not the answer to all our problems, nor the only way to make peace. Civil disobedience is a way to raise questions; one way among many to make peace; one way to respond to the pressing moral and spiritual issues of war, injustice, the climate emergency and systemic violence.

When engaged in a spirit of love, truth, faith and community, nonviolent action can be a way for God's Spirit to move in our world, a way for us to withdraw our consent from the wars and injustices of the age. With such tremendous spiritual potential at stake, it is essential to approach civil disobedience with great care, in a spirit of prayer, discernment and preparation.

Those who engage in civil disobedience should be people who have committed their lives to the search for justice and peace. We should be people rooted in prayer, nonviolence, contemplation, faith in the God of peace, hope, charity, kindness, humility, joy, service, community, and solidarity with the poor. As we consider an act of civil disobedience, we should test the levels of nonviolence in our hearts and community and pray for God's blessing on the action, the

---

* When civil disobedience is performed out of a compulsive spirit and is not rooted in a prayer of love, then problems rooted in violence and confusion will arise.

community, and all those who will witness it or be involved in it in whatever way.

Our attitude must be truly nonviolent, free of self-righteousness, elitism, or judgment of others. As the Pax Christi guidelines on civil disobedience observe, "One way of witness [such as civil disobedience] does not enjoy moral or spiritual superiority over other ways. Everyone does what they can according to the call of God and their special gifts."[1]

If our civil disobedience arises only from anger, and is sustained only by our anger—not our love—then perhaps we should not participate in the action. Civil disobedience requires more than anger at our unjust system. It must be rooted in love—indeed, the love of God—if it is to become sacramental and thus transformational. We must redirect and transcend our anger so that we become signs of God's love and grace moving in our world. Acting in this spirit will require discernment, preparation, and a serious pursuit of spiritual growth in nonviolence.

As Christians, we are always trying to witness to the truth and love of God. Thus, our actions must be rooted in love. St. Paul's famous Scripture passage is worth keeping in mind in the context of our civil disobedience: "if I have all faith so as to move mountains but do not have love, I am nothing. If I give away everything I own, and if I hand my body over to be burned but do not have love, I gain nothing" (1 Cor. 13:1-8).

We could add, "If I am arrested for an act of civil disobedience and spend years in prison, but have not love,

I have wasted my time." This underlying spirit of love is essential in our acts of civil disobedience, otherwise we should not participate in them. If our civil disobedience is not rooted in nonviolent love—ideally, the love of God— then we have learned nothing about peacemaking and need to start all over again.

Writer and social critic Jack Nelson-Pallmeyer once said in an interview that "in some instances, people are choosing the option of jail from a place of hardness of heart rather than a place of compassion. They find it easier to survive in that atmosphere than they do in talking to their neighbors and in dealing with the discrepancy between where their neighbors are and the urgency they themselves feel."[2]

If our action is to be sacramental, Godly, spirit-filled, then our willingness to go to jail must come from a disarmed heart filled with love for all people, *especially* those engaged in the injustice we oppose. Peace activist and Benedictine sister Mary Lou Kownacki has written, "It's easier and more glamorous for me to get arrested at the White House than to hold a house meeting on the [nuclear] threat in my Aunt Louise's living room."

"Acceptance of suffering," she continues, "can be a proof of love, [but] it can also demonstrate hardness of heart." The distinction comes in the way we treat our "so-called opponent"—showing them love, and trust, even when they have wronged us twenty times. "An implicit trust in human nature is the very essence of [the Christian's] creed."

Prayer, Kownacki concludes, must be the bedrock of the nonviolent community. If prayer is missing (or infrequent) in the preparation process, then we should be worried:

> If the only time one's peace community prays is before
> a protest action, then some serious questions need to
> be raised... That could be an exercise in self-deception,
> using prayer to convince ourselves that what we do is
> inspired by God. Prayer should be regular and constant,
> always open to God's will."[3]

Testing our motivations

Civil disobedience can be done in an unhealthy spirit, for the wrong reasons. How do we prevent this from happening? Through prayer, discernment, self-examination, communal discussion, and a constant deepening of our spirits in the nonviolent, unconditional love of God.

The Pax Christi statement on civil disobedience explains that we must be spiritually prepared for civil disobedience:

> Because we are a responsible people, we believe
> legitimate civil disobedience can and must include a
> whole spectrum of activities: protest and persuasion,
> forms of non-cooperation and symbolic actions. In an
> effort to discern what forms of civil disobedience are
> appropriate, there can and will be honest disagreement.
> Concrete tactics are subject to many variables. The
> whole issue of what is an effective nonviolent symbol
> can be complex.

What is absolutely crucial is that such an issue be discussed openly, freely, prayerfully. The tradition of Christian discernment includes some testing of spirits even in the context of the larger Eucharistic community. Discernment demands a rigorous detachment from vested interests of any kind.[4]

If we are going to remain nonviolent and loving, we must examine the motives behind our interest in civil disobedience to see that we are rooted in the love of God. We must continually discern the spirits involved in our acts of civil disobedience to see if they are truly right, if they are 'of God'. We must first, then, be discerning people, attuned to the Spirit of God at work in our hearts and in our world.

How do we know if God is inviting us into an act of nonviolent civil disobedience or not? How do we know if this is God's will for us? How do we know whether or not our participation in such a public display is of God or of some evil spirit? How do we discern our participation in an act of civil disobedience as God's will for us? What questions should we ask ourselves and our fellow participants? How do we find God's will in the first place? How will we know if God's Spirit is moving in us, calling us forward into the risk of active nonviolence?

In particular, what are our motivations behind such an act? Is our participation a compulsive response that originates in a *lack* of freedom; a manifestation of our domineering egos and violence; an unhealthy addiction that is avoiding the serious spiritual turmoil in our own souls? These are questions we need to grapple with whenever we consider, prepare for, and engage in civil disobedience, if we want our nonviolent action to be sacramental.

Such questions were acutely tested at a peacemaking retreat in Washington, DC, in May, 1986. A gathering of Jesuits and friends had been called "to discern God's Spirit of peacemaking." Some 75 of us met in the basement of St. Aloysius' Church, five blocks north of the US Capitol, for prayer and discussion on three issues: the US wars in Central America, the US nuclear arsenal, and homelessness.

Each day featured a presentation by a Christian peacemaker deeply involved in those struggles: Jean Walsh, who spoke of her work with Witness for Peace, a project that sent people to stand in solidarity with our Nicaraguan brothers and sisters on the Honduran border as they faced the US-backed contras; Daniel Berrigan, who spoke of disarmament and the Plowshares movement; and Ned Murphy, who spoke of his work with the homeless and the hungry in New York City.

After each day's prayer, presentation and discussion, we held a vigil outside a focal point of those issues: at the US Capitol, where debate continued on funding the Contras and the Salvadoran death-squad government; at the Pentagon, where strategies for nuclear warfare were being drawn up; and at the White House, where all these polices of death were coordinated and set in stone, ensuring the continuation of the sufferings of the homeless poor throughout the nation and the world.

At some point, we decided that some of us would engage in nonviolent civil disobedience on the final day of our retreat by kneeling in a prayer for peace in front of the White House. For many, this event would be the first time they had ever vigilled and held a peace sign, much less risked arrest in an act of civil disobedience. For myself, it would be a prayerful moment to state publicly our opposition as church people to the US policies which kill the poor. As I soon discovered, there were other motives involved.

The conversations went on long into the night. After our initial prayer, those of us who felt moved to risk an act of civil disobedience explained our reasons for such a protest. After sixteen people had spoken, we discussed possible scenarios and decided to kneel in prayer in front of the White House. We talked about the various outcomes and pledged to keep an open mind and attitude towards one another as the event unfolded, in case some chose to withdraw from the action. We committed ourselves to act together as a community in a nonviolent spirit. If some decision needed to be made, we would act together as a peacemaking community.

The next morning, after Eucharist, we processed to Lafayette Park across the street from the White House, where we formed a circle and offered prayers on behalf of all those suffering under systemic violence. Then, the sixteen of us who had prepared, walked across Pennsylvania Avenue and knelt down in silent prayer directly in front of the White House. After a short while, we sat down and sang hymns to the God of peace.

Just then, the sprinkler system for the front lawn of the White House was suddenly turned on (in order to deter us from staying any longer, we believed). Since it was unbearably hot and humid, we did not mind the refreshing shower. Some fifteen reporters and TV camera people closed in on us to film our action. As the minutes ticked away, it became clear that the White House police were reluctant to arrest us, possibly because of the large press coverage that we would receive. Instead, a police officer told us that since we were not wearing signs or holding a banner (as our supporters were in the nearby legal vigil area), we would not be arrested.

It was then that a new round of community discernment began, an experience which left me initially confused and bewildered. We formed a circle and asked each other what we should do next. We had pledged to act together in community and to talk out our response. Since we had agreed to pray in front of the White House and not necessarily to wear a sign or be arrested, most people felt that we should conclude with a song and return to the church. Our witness had been complete, it was suggested. I gently disagreed, observing that we could easily borrow one of the beautiful banners from the legal vigillers and make a witness that would risk arrest, a stronger statement than our legal kneel-in.

What should we do? In this unplanned moment, we entered deeper than we had expected into the theme of our retreat, *Discerning the Spirit's Call to Peacemaking*. We decided as a group to remain seated for a half hour of silent prayer followed by a process of communal decision-making to which everyone would agree. And so, we sat in silence in front of the White House.

The other vigillers continued to hold their signs, while the press talked to one another awaiting our response. When the time was up, the near unanimous agreement was reached to conclude the action. It appeared to me that I was the only person who wanted to risk arrest, but since I had agreed to abide by the Spirit of the group, I did not take a sign and provoke arrest, but joined everyone in a closing prayer for peace with justice.

I ended the retreat confused and bewildered as well as struck by the Spirit of God moving among the newborn community of nonviolent resisters. Following the prayerful discernment made in community, I had to put aside my own ego, will and ambition for a peaceful act of civil disobedience that resulted in arrest, and walk humbly with the community. I came to realize that there were other motives behind my desire—such as the egocentric goal of concluding a successful retreat, which I had helped organize, with a high profile action that would impress people. In our communal discernment, I learned to trust in the Spirit of God moving in the group. I learned that our motives are never pure, but that through common sharing and a prayerful search, we can live up to our calling and be more rooted in nonviolence and the Spirit of God, if we only let God take the lead.

In the end, I realized that the Spirit of peace was moving among us and that those days would bear great fruit in the lives of all who participated. The discernment was painful for me; I did not do what I personally wanted the group to do. And yet, I now see that the right decision had been made by the group, that it was better to let go of my own control and enter the communal struggle to follow the lead of the Spirit. This experience proved to be enlightening, liberating and life-giving. The Spirit seemed to move in freedom among us.

Civil disobedience can only be sacramental, I believe, when we enter into the act with a humble spirit that has discerned and reflected on God's will for one's self and humanity. The conditions for such civil disobedience can best be set in place when it is conceived in the life-context of spiritual discernment and prayerful reflection. One should act in response to an inner voice, from a sense of being called; then the action will bear fruit for the long haul of salvation and peace.

Ignatian discernment and peacemaking

St. Ignatius Loyola, the founder of the Society of Jesus, outlined a series of suggestions to help with the discernment of spirits so that we might do God's will. His guidelines may be helpful in our preparation for sacramental civil disobedience. They presuppose a life of regular prayer, communal worship, and spiritual direction (with someone skilled in the art of discernment).

Ignatius points out that the good spirit works in two different ways, depending on what he calls, "our state in life." If we are "complacent, apathetic, or lazy" regarding the spiritual life, the evil spirit will fill our imaginations with "sensual delights" or "worldly thoughts" so that we do not change the direction of our lives. In this mindset, the good spirit comes and "stings our conscience" to wake us up to do God's will.

If, on the other hand, we are intent upon doing God's will all the days of our life, with all our energy and strength, the evil spirit will raise every variety of difficulty, filling us with anxieties, worries, and obstacles in order to discourage us. In this situation, the good spirit "strengthens, encourages, consoles, and inspires us" to move us to a firm resolve.

Pursuing holiness and God's will "gives delight and joy, and no obstacle seems to be so formidable that it cannot be faced and overcome," writes St. Ignatius.[5] Accordingly, for years, the good spirit may prick our consciences to take the risk of an act of civil disobedience.

If such an action is rooted in nonviolence, community and God's Spirit, then as we set our sights on such an action and resolve to commit ourselves to participate in it with an attentive, prayerful spirit, the good spirit will try to encourage us, and overcome the evil spirit's effort to confuse us. In this setting, we must be aware of the movement of God's spirit, encouraging us and calling us forward to do God's will. With practice, we can learn to be attuned to the Holy Spirit and this disposition can help us in our public witness.

Spiritual discernment has been defined simply as recognising the differences in the spirits moving inside us and discovering which spirit is from God.[6] One good way to search our hearts in a discerning mode is to compare our experience in prayer as we consider an act of civil disobedience with some prayerful experience we have had in which we are sure that the Spirit of God was present. A regular habit of praying, talking with and listening to God will aid us if we want to be discerning people. We will learn to ask God in prayer if God wants us to participate in an act of nonviolent civil disobedience, and to listen for God's response.

We must ask to see our participation in civil disobedience from God's perspective, through God's grace, and discover where our motives need to be purified. We can ask God about our motives for engaging in civil disobedience and we must diligently seek God's response: Is God affirming us, encouraging us to participate in civil disobedience as a way to proclaim God's reign of nonviolent love, or is God saying something else?

What does the Jesus of the Gospels say to us as we meditate on the Scriptures—and imagine ourselves with Jesus, discussing our nonviolence and the risk of civil disobedience? Do we feel peace and inner freedom in God's affirmation of our participation in civil disobedience? In other words, do we see and feel the signs of God's presence among us as we enter into this act from our prayer? Do we find the fruits of the Spirit in our discernment and preparation? As St. Paul wrote, "the fruit of the Spirit is love, joy, peace, patience, kindness, goodness, faithfulness, gentleness, self-control" (Gal. 5:22-23).

There are many questions to consider when one is discerning an act of civil disobedience. A simple checklist of questions to be prayed through in our discernment might then include some of the following themes:

Ten questions for reflection

One:

Does God want me to participate in this act of nonviolent civil disobedience? Is this act initiated by God; is it part of God's will? Am I centered in a faithful obedience to the God of peace and justice, so that first and foremost, obedience to God's will (and thus the love of humanity) is my primary concern?

Two:

What exactly are my motives for engaging in the act? With deep honesty, list the various reasons for participating in this act, and the various reasons against participating in this act. Do the positives outweigh the negatives, or are there any negatives which in conscience forbids me from participating in this act of civil disobedience? Do the negatives reveal that I have to take more time in praying and preparing for this act of civil disobedience?

Three:

In particular, would my not performing civil disobedience manifest continued moral complicity or acquiescence in evil? Does the action as such represent my non-complicity in what I judge as morally evil? Does the action intend to influence public policy by arousing public support; raise significant ethical questions; or invite others to reflect upon their complicity in what I regard as morally evil?

Four:

How much trust am I placing in God? What do the Scriptures invite me to do in this situation? How would Jesus have responded to this situation? When I contemplate being with the Jesus of the Gospels, and ask him if he wants me to take part in this act of nonviolent civil disobedience, what does he say to me? Do I place too much concern on how others might misunderstand my action (and thus reject me) or on the political efficacy of the action itself, and not on the inherent truthfulness within the nonviolence?

Five:

Are the other participants committed to nonviolence? Is this group seeking to do God's will; that is, are they seeking to witness to the nonviolent love and peace of God the Creator? Does this action keep within the spirit of the sacramental civil disobedience practiced by Dr. Martin Luther King Jr., Dorothy Day, Gandhi and other models of nonviolent resistance?

Six:

Does my faith require me to participate in this action at this time? Would it be an omission on my part, indeed, would it be morally wrong not to participate in this action?

Seven:

Are we acting out of anger or a self-righteous, judgmental spirit? Are we acting out of fear, and if so, are we willing to share our fears with others? How can I be disarmed of this anger, self-righteousness or fear?

Eight:

How does the social context within which I am discerning, living, and making decisions about peacemaking affect the kind of decisions and activities that I participate in?

Nine:

What kind of risky nonviolence is God calling us to, we must ask? If I am a young Palestinian in Gaza or the West Bank and I am considering an act of nonviolent civil disobedience, I may very well be risking my life in such an action. Even in Europe or the United States, if I am a person of color, I may well be treated very harshly by the police during a demonstration or during the process of arrest, as compared with being white and middle class.*

Am I in tune with the spiritual currents and consequences of my nonviolent action? Can I consider a risky nonviolence, such as a Plowshares Action, that might lead to years in prison? Why might I be reluctant to consider an action? Could the God who led Jesus to risk arrest and crucifixion through a life of active civil disobedience that culminated

---

* This issue has been particularly highlighted since the murder of George Floyd in 2020 and the rise of Black Lives Matter. If I am white and middle class in a western country, my risk will probably not involve a long-term prison sentence, nor torture nor physical death, but only the symbolic statement of opposing injustice and systemic violence. There may be few physical consequences.

in Jerusalem with 'the Temple action,' be inviting me to such an act of nonviolent resistance?

Ten:

How prepared am I to go to jail and to trial? Have I discussed this action with my community and my family and taken their lives into consideration?

•

Questions such as these seek to get at the root spirit within one's heart as one prepares for an act of civil disobedience. They can help turn the focus of the action on God and God's action in one's own heart and soul and in the world. When they are explored in prayer with total honesty before God, they allow the light of God's love to fall on our motives and dispositions. In this light, we can grow spiritually and be purified of all that holds us back from God's own unconditional love: our anger, hostility, egoism, bitterness, resentment, broken relations with others, hatred, violence, sexism, racism, dominating will, and judgment of others.

When we enter into this purifying process of prayerful preparation before an act of civil disobedience, and discern how God is moving us to act publicly in this way for God's peace—then we can go forward with the action in a spirit of prayer, humility, peace, confidence and deep joy knowing that we are doing God's will. When we engage in a discerned sacramental act of civil disobedience, we can then be contemplatives as well as prophets of peace.

If we want our participation in civil disobedience to be sacramental, it must flow from a life of prayer and contemplation in which such questions can be freely asked and faced. It is particularly helpful to have someone to talk with regularly about our spiritual life: a spiritual director who can help us to notice where God is present and acting in our lives, and what God is saying to us.

Ideally, then, any discerning spirit who engages in civil disobedience also takes time off in life to reflect and pray intensely—whether in a monastery, retreat centre or out in the wilderness—so that the upcoming action is truly rooted in God, and a life committed to God. In such a life, the act of civil disobedience is merely one more step in a daily journey to Christian discipleship and faithfulness.

The key to remember in the process of spiritual discernment is to move away from our conformity to this world and to be conformed to Christ; to put on the mind and heart of Christ; to keep going back to the Scriptures and allow our lives to fit into the peacemaking stories of the Scriptures, so that we truly become modern-day disciples of Jesus.

We must keep asking ourselves: are we growing in our faith and maturing in our discipleship with Jesus? Or, to paraphrase St. Ignatius: What have we done for the peacemaking Christ; what are we doing for the peacemaking Christ; and what are we going to do for the peacemaking Christ?

Practical preparation for an act of nonviolent civil disobedience

Civil disobedience can be sacramental when it is prepared well, and thought-out ahead of time, in a reflective spirit of love. Besides the prayerful, individual and communal discernment that should proceed any sacramental civil disobedience, careful preparation is necessary for the scenario itself.*

Forming the community of peacemakers

In the spiritual crisis of social injustice, we speak through nonviolent direct action on the symbolic level to society as a whole, to awaken the conscience within us as individuals, as nations and as an interdependent world community. Our creative acts should state our position clearly and touch the hearts of others in a spirit of love.

At the heart of this process is the formation of community among those engaged in the action, so that the spirit of the witness will continue through the consequences of arrest, court hearings and even jail or prison. It is always beneficial to build community, not only to model 'the beloved community' that we are proclaiming, but to ensure that no one undergoes the action on their own without support from others.

---

* Not simply to restrain spontaneous self-expression that could diffuse the focus of the action, but to ensure that the spirit of love can truly be set free in the witness and encounter with one's opponents.

It is best to act in an affinity group or a community of friends that has already been formed. Otherwise, people should spend some time sharing their faith journeys and life stories with one another. In this process, everyone should be able to tell each other what it is that has moved them to take this step, to cross the line in an act of civil disobedience. The personal, private discernment that has preceded the action can be shared in the community so that the community itself can respond as a corporate body, and thus be united in prayer and spirit for the action itself.

It is important to state this: in large public demonstrations, the entire community of nonviolent resisters, including the legal supporters, together make the witness for peace. Those risking arrest must not judge those who do not participate in the civil disobedience, and those who do not participate in the civil disobedience but join in a supporting vigil, must freely allow those risking arrest to discuss their action, their response to unforeseen circumstances, and the follow up their action will require. Together, the prayerful, peaceful witness will send a strong signal of love that has the potential to transform others as well as ourselves.

In this spirit of community, we will be better able to maintain a prayerful joyful spirit of nonviolent love, and respect for our adversaries, as we go forth in our witness for peace. We will be able to stay focused on Christ because of this support, drawing spiritual strength from each other. We will be able to sustain that Spirit of love as we encounter police officers, counter-demonstrators, military or government employees, lawyers, judges and prison guards.

Perhaps no group prepares more for sacramental civil disobedience than those communities of resisters in the Plowshares movement who enter nuclear installations to 'beat nuclear swords into plowshares of peace.' The prospect of entering an arms factory or military base, and damaging a missile cone, requires a prolonged process of decision-making. Some groups prepare together for as long as two years, knowing that some activists have received prison sentences of up to eighteen years.

Sister Anne Montgomery, who has spent over two and a half years in jail for her participation in the Plowshares Eight, the Trident Nein Plowshares and the Pershing Plowshares actions in the United States, outlines their process of preparation for peaceful civil disobedience in her book, *Swords into Plowshares*.

The process begins with prayer and reflection, making decisions together as a community. "We try to reach a harmony," Montgomery writes, "deeper than differences in philosophy and style." Establishing this relationship now is crucial; that spirit must be maintained through the trial and prison processes, which are much more difficult conditions for reaching consensus together.

Depth and relationship, she emphasizes, are more important than numbers, or high-powered organization. This is central to making their prayer and action one, and to reaching out to the 'other' in a truly personal way. The Plowshares, then, examine together their attitudes towards the very court officers, police, military, and arms workers that they will encounter in their action, "reminding ourselves that we are bound together by our responsibility for violence, as well as our desire that life be protected." They pray that the fears and hopes which confrontation brings to the surface (on both sides) will lead to a mutual understanding and healing.

However desirable it may seem to have the power of the media, or strength in numbers, Montgomery adds, "our weakness is our strength, for it leaves us trusting in the power of God." As Gandhi has said, the means and the end are "contained together in the seed our witness plants." The action, in itself, tips the balance in the world, however subtly: "if it is a community action, there is [now] more community in the world; if it is a repentant action, there is already more reconciliation." She continues:

> The Gospel promise of "greater works" is to those who believe. We must be responsible and do our homework, research and choose our site with care, reflect and pray over the pros and cons of the action and symbols, and open up channels of support and feasibility. Then the moment of speaking the truth becomes a leap of faith that opens us to the power of that truth.[7]

Over the months of preparations, the acting community makes weekend retreats on a variety of themes. They share their life stories; study the Scriptures, particularly the second chapter of Isaiah and the life of Jesus; analyze the facts of our nuclear arsenal and militarism; explore their understanding of nonviolence; confess their fears; discuss the scenario; write a statement about why they are acting; and learn to keep a spirit of peace while in jail.

They also examine the risks and the obstacles in both the planned action, and the possible consequences of long prison sentences, or even accident or death. These must be considered in light of the potential effect on other relationships and responsibilities in the activists' lives. All must "work through [their] convictions and feelings concerning court and jail proceedings."

> Finally, when research and reason have reached a certain point, before an action that seems "right", there is usually a moment, or series of moments, hard to describe, of "coming together" of community and action, of time and place, a moment of "seeing through a glass darkly", yet with the sureness of faith. We are not sure everything will turn out perfectly, but we are sure that it is right to go ahead. We will stop if violence threatens, but we are sure, too, that the doors meant to open will do so.

> Whether or not the physical ones do so, the community action itself is an opening of a door, a step into freedom and a prayer for the intervention of mercy in history, for we refuse to believe that we are walled into fatalistic cycles of war or oppression or destined for holocaust. Above all, we are certain that the whole point of the process is our obedience and that the results are in the hands of God. [8]

Making a covenant of nonviolence

To focus our commitment to nonviolence, I recommend that sacramental civil disobedience should include a 'covenant of nonviolence' written out, reflected over and agreed to in advance, especially if the participants have gathered together for the first time before the action or do not know one another well.

From the Sojourners Community in Washington, DC, to the Nuremberg Actions Community in Concord, California, peace communities across the United States and elsewhere have found this process valuable in active nonviolence. They covenant themselves to the spirit and practice of nonviolence before every act of civil disobedience.

For example, when a group of university students organized a sit-in to protest CIA recruitment at their school, they studied the nonviolent covenants used by Gandhi, King and others, and wrote their own contract of nonviolence:

We covenant together to abide by the following disciplines of nonviolence in thought, word, and deed:

1. *Meditate on the life and teachings of Jesus, the Prince of Peace.*

2. *Pray to be used by the Holy Spirit as channels of peace, justice and goodwill.*

3. *Do not engage in violence of fist, tongue or heart. Carry no weapons. Do not kill or injure. Refrain from insulting remarks.*

4. *Walk and talk in a prayerful spirit of peace and love, for "God is Love," so that we might be channels of God's peace and love.*

5. *Carry symbols that convey love and respect, not hostility. Remember that nonviolence seeks justice and reconciliation not victory.*

6. *Be open, friendly, and respectful toward all including police officers, security guards and other officials. Observe with everyone the ordinary rules of courtesy.*

7. *Pray for any opponents and protect them from insult or attack. We will harbor no hate. Should others express violence toward us, we will ask that the violence be stopped and not return violence with violence.*

8. *If arrested, go peacefully and act with dignity and love.*

9. *Do not bring or use any drugs or alcohol other than for medical purposes.*

10. *Follow the directions of designated spokespersons. In the event of a serious disagreement, one should remove oneself from the action.*

11. *We will show respect for the police. We will not evade the consequences of our actions. If arrested, we will go peacefully and act with dignity and love. If we are not arrested, we will not deviate from the agreed upon scenario merely to provoke arrest. We will be alert to the people around us and will be aware when others need assistance. We will support each other in needs for peacekeeping.*[9]

The articulation of these basic principles of nonviolence before each and every act of civil disobedience will help us to remember the Spirit we wish to convey and the attitude that we want to have at all times. Since nonviolence is a way of life that takes our entire lives to learn, such basic covenants will always help ensure a peaceful tone. Some of us have even pledged vows of nonviolence to keep us ever reflecting on the need for disarmed hearts.[10]

Thinking through the action

Good preparation will entail investigating the area beforehand and charting out exactly how the action can take place. As part of our preparation, especially for actions involving a large number of people or the possibility of a violent response by the police, it will help to rehearse and dramatize the event beforehand, just as liturgists practice and rehearse liturgies, wedding ceremonies and other sacraments prior to the actual event.

Those who are planning to engage in the civil disobedience should role-play the action ahead of time, and practice their nonviolent response in various scenarios. Peaceful symbols and signs need to be made or arranged ahead of time as well. As we prepare, we must discipline ourselves to be respectful of others at all times and open to the truth within our adversaries. We must check the consistency of our nonviolence in our messages, symbols, acts, words and hearts. Within the community of resisters, we can test our nonviolence and brainstorm for more creative nonviolence.

As we think through an action, we should talk it over with the significant family and community members in our lives, if possible. We should plan how our family and community responsibilities will be met if we are detained or imprisoned because of our action. Some married activists take turns participating in acts of civil disobedience so that both parents do not end up in jail at the same time and so that one parent is always available for the children and the other for the action.

We also need to reflect and discuss our participation in civil disobedience and how that will fit in with and conflict with our other community, ministry, and/or employment commitments. We need to be thoughtful and yet open to the movement of the Holy Spirit. Prayerful discernment, as always, is crucial.

It may prove helpful as well to prepare beforehand a statement that makes clear the reasons for our nonviolent activity. Lawyers might be contacted to get a sense of the legal ramifications of our civil disobedience, especially if there is a serious possibility of spending several months or years in prison.

With large numbers of people, sign up sheets should be passed around so that people can be contacted after the event to prepare for court appearances.

Many activists follow the Gandhian tradition of telling the local police beforehand that civil disobedience will occur in the hope that the police will respond nonviolently and perhaps one day cooperate in the campaign of nonviolence itself to help transform the situation.

If possible, before the action, groups can share with each other how they may respond to the consequences: by paying a fine or refusing to pay any fine or bail; by non-cooperating with the police by not giving one's name; by pleading guilty or not guilty; or by refusing to take probation or to do community service for a higher principle.

Arrangements should be made ahead of time for supporters and friends to check on those arrested, to take them home from jail or to find out where they have been taken.

Finally, it is beneficial to take time after the action to reflect together on the experience and to critique it, as well as to celebrate the witness!

Northern Ireland's Peace People have outlined several points to keep in mind in preparing for nonviolent action:

1. *Be clear about one's objectives. They must be reasonable, realizable and specific. The nonviolent action should not aim too high. The practical objectives should be thought out ahead of time, and may even be communicated to the opponent ahead of time.*

2. *Don't be frightened. Fear is perceived, and encourages the opponent to continue the undesired activity. It is difficult not to be afraid in a confrontation, but not impossible. Breathe deeply, keep talking slowly. Maintain eye contact without challenging the opponent.*

3. *Don't be frightening. Someone about to commit an act of violence is likely to be more fearful than the person being attacked. Make no abrupt gestures. Move slowly. Don't say anything threatening, critical or hostile.*

4. *Try to clarify the situation. Don't hesitate to state the obvious. It helps and sometimes can have amazing results. A demonstrator being dragged by his hair looked up at the policeman and said, "You're pulling my hair and it hurts." This got through to the policeman, who released the hair and began dragging the demonstrator by his arms instead.*

5. *Don't behave like a victim. Someone in the process of committing an act of violence has strong expectations of how the victim will behave. Behaving differently, in a non-threatening manner, can interrupt the flow of events and avoid an act of violence.*

6. *Seek to befriend your opponent's better nature. This is at the heart of nonviolent action. Even the most brutal and brutalized have some spark of decency which the nonviolent person can reach. The task is to help the opponent see that the intended act of violence is inconsistent with the kind of person the opponent wishes to be.*

7. *Be firm in the face of physical violence. The most frequent mistake nonviolent persons make is that they do not resist firmly enough. They should be outgoing. Passivity usually further angers a violent person. But sometimes an opponent is so upset that even a mild form of resistance can be explosive. It has to be played by ear. The best rule is to resist as firmly as possible without escalating the anger or the violence.*

8. *Get the opponent talking. Don't argue but at the same time don't give the impression of agreeing with assertions that are cruel or immoral. The listening is more important than what is said. Keep the talk going and keep it calm.*[11]

With spiritual discernment and practical preparation, civil disobedience can be an act of hope for the world and a sign of God's love that touches a nerve in humanity, transforming our world through God's grace. As a new sacrament, it can enable the grace of God to witness for peace in the world by opening up a channel in the public arena for the spirit of nonviolent love to be unleashed so that the hearts of many can be touched. It can truly be sacramental. But the nonviolent witness does not end there: it continues through the consequences of the action, in the court proceedings and the jail sentences.

the opportunity for ██████████████ in the situation.

███████████████████████████████████████
███████████████████████████████████████
███████████████████████████████████████

████████████████████ and so now preparation.
████████████████████████████ the world and
███████████████████████ one has a place in it depends
considerably on whether one has a chance to give expression to one's reality and a place to give one
form to the world by producing a world that matters
both for the self and for another. It will be in this
domain that relatedness and betweenness can truly be
distinguished. But the boundaries between them, though
there, is continuous through the consequences of these
being experienced as if time has no influence.

EIGHT

Anything Can Happen

Accepting the consequences with gratitude and love

No one can ever say for sure what the outcome of our sacramental civil disobedience will be. No matter how much experience, how much consultation, or how many prior arrests, events can easily change course and turn in a direction we never anticipated.

A key factor in our sacramental civil disobedience therefore will be preparing for a wide variety of consequences, placing those consequences in God's hands, letting go of our anxieties and control, trusting in God, and walking forward in a spirit of peace and love. In that spirit, then, we will be able to accept whatever the consequences of our action turn out to be as a blessing and a gift from God.

In this spirit, we can have new eyes to see the transforming grace at work among us no matter what the outcome. We will be able to appreciate better the sacramentality of the moment and be transformed ourselves. Whether we are arrested and released, arrested and imprisoned for years, or not arrested at all for our civil disobedience, we will trust in the Spirit's presence among us in our witness, and know that God's love is at work in ways we may not even be able to imagine.

One consequence may indeed include the transformation of injustice to justice. We must stay rooted in the spiritual depths of our civil disobedience so that we will be able to receive the spiritual consequences of our sacramental action. We need to learn to trust in the goodness and the truth of the nonviolence itself, and that our public nonviolence will proclaim the greater glory of God and the coming of God's reign of justice and peace in our world.

Plowshares activists in the United States and elsewhere have learned these hard lessons through years of practice, and they trust that God's grace will be present in the action. They have experienced a wide variety of consequences for their actions.

Before the first Plowshares action, a lawyer told the Plowshares Eight that "they would never walk away from the action," meaning that they might be imprisoned for life. Though some were jailed for many months, in the end, after a series of appeals, they were sentenced to time served. On the other hand, the Silo-Pruning Hooks were sentenced for up to eighteen years in prison, and indeed have spent many years there. The AEGIS Plowshares, who hammered on the USS. Gettysburg on Easter Sunday, 1991, had their charges lowered to misdemeanors.

Whenever we participate in public nonviolence that risks arrest, we must be prepared for any and every possible outcome, from arrest and long term imprisonment; to physical violence and even death; to *not* being arrested, and being ignored.

The lessons of civil disobedience in our world history point to a greater need for preparation when undertaking nonviolent civil disobedience. The world saw this in June, 1989, when after months of nonviolent student demonstrations in Beijing, the Chinese military opened fire and killed hundreds of students, to the shock of the world.

On May 21, 1930, when hundreds of Gandhian independence demonstrators walked forward to enter the Dharasana salt works to protest unjust salt laws and British domination of India, they were beaten over the head with steel rods. They suffered fractured skulls, broken bones and serious internal injuries. Several people died from their wounds. The violence they experienced was perhaps not what they expected, although they knew it was a possibility; but their nonviolent response captured the imagination of the world and paved the way for India's independence. They were deeply trained in the spiritual and practical roots of sacramental nonviolence and thus the outcome bore fruit, as Jesus showed it could in the way he prepared for and died on the cross.

Similarly, when Brian Willson and several others sat on train tracks outside the entrance to the Concord Naval Weapons Station in California on September 1, 1987, in order to block train shipments of bombs headed for Central America, they anticipated being arrested and jailed. Instead, the train sped up and ran over Brian Willson. Miraculously, he was not killed, but he lost both legs and suffered a severe head injury. His forgiving spirit inspired people throughout the nation to stand up and speak out against the US war with Nicaragua.

No matter what the consequences are, sacramental civil disobedience can bear miraculous fruit. When Rosa Parks refused to give up her seat in the back of a bus on December 1, 1955, she suspected she would be arrested, but she never dreamed her resistance would spark a national movement and affect the history of the world. The consequences of her nonviolence were both real and concrete—she went to jail for the evening—and unexpected and earth-shaking, for she ignited a nonviolent revolution, a lightning fire of nonviolence.

Rosa Parks' action was continued by the Freedom Riders, who at great cost to themselves, boarded buses—black and white sitting together, when this was illegal—and travelled to the far south of the US into the heart of segregation country. They were brutally beaten, and ended up hospitalised for their severe injuries. Immediately, another group of black and white citizens repeated the action until finally the racist segregation on the buses ceased.

Similarly, Dorothy Day and the Catholic Workers who sat down on park benches in New York City in the late 1950s and early 1960s during nuclear war air-raid "defense" drills, finally impressed the nation with the foolishness of such exercises and put an end to the drills, as well as raising awareness about the nuclear nightmare.

Two of the four ANZUS Plowshares, who had entered Griffiss Airbase outside Rome, New York, on New Year's Day, 1991, cut through fences marked 'Deadly Force Zone'. The two activists, Bill and Sue Frankel-Streit, literally risked their lives, for the police had been trained to shoot to kill. Yet in a spirit of courageous love that overcame their fears, they went forward and were able to hammer on a B-52 bomber and mark it with peace signs.

Likewise, we might not even be arrested, no matter how hard we try; or we might be arrested when we have not planned to be. Once, I joined a demonstration outside the Israeli consulate in New York City to protest the Israeli violence towards the Palestinians. Along with ten other friends, I fully expected to be arrested.

Because there were some well-known people among our group, scores of press people appeared as well as a swarm of police officers to watch our sit-in. I stood on the edge of the group, when suddenly, just as my friends sat down, the press crowded in on us and the police started making arrests. In the commotion that followed, as police officers jostled press people to arrest the well-known activists, I was cut off from the group.

In the mix up, I found myself suddenly all alone as my friends were loaded into police vans and whisked away, and the press people disappeared. I approached one police officer and said, "I'm with the demonstrators. I was committing the civil disobedience, too." He replied, "That's okay. We're not interested in you." I was left on my own, and very disappointed that I had not been arrested.

On another occasion, in April of 1989, I was supporting a group of ten nonviolent demonstrators as they sat in a hallway on the fifth floor of the District Building in Washington, DC, where the Mayor's Office and the City Council Chambers are located. Along with hundreds of homeless people, we were protesting the city council's plans to abolish a referendum/law requiring the city to shelter every homeless person.

My friends sat on the floor and sang very loudly, causing a loud disturbance. Hundreds of people milled about the huge hallway, but only those ten people sitting on the floor were breaking the law. I stood at one end of the long hallway, several hundred feet away from the demonstrators being interviewed by a reporter about homelessness, when suddenly a police officer grabbed my arm, pulled me into an elevator and placed me under arrest!

I had not prepared to go to jail, since I had a busy schedule that day back at the shelter for the homeless where I worked. Despite my pleas of innocence, I was whisked off to jail with the ten demonstrators. We were held until late in the evening, and had to appear in court the next morning —and several times afterwards for arraignment.

When a judge dismissed the charges against us, the DC government appealed and sought to bring me to trial. The experience gave me a short taste of life on the streets for homeless people, who are often the victims of police harassment and illegal arrest. I also learned to be prepared for anything whenever I join in a legal vigil to support those risking arrest. It is not uncommon for police officers to round up bystanders in order to discourage public demonstrations of any kind.

The possibilities and surprising consequences of sacramental civil disobedience first became apparent to me in April 1984, when I blocked a doorway at the Pentagon by myself in an act of nonviolent civil disobedience. I had followed what I thought was the invitation of the Spirit to express publicly my resistance to the nuclear policies of the United States; even though, at the time, I was a novice in the Society of Jesus, and had been warned not to participate in civil disobedience. Such an action on my part, I was told, would lead to my dismissal from the Jesuit Order, a consequence which I found greatly disturbing and very upsetting.

Through years of discernment, I had felt called by God to a lifetime of service in the Jesuit community and a lifetime of active peacemaking that would include the risk of peaceful civil disobedience. My action was a prayerful experiment to live out what I thought was God's call. Though I felt God inviting me to both vocations (which I saw as one vocation), my community superiors told me that I had to make a choice. Pushed by the Spirit of God, I went forward in the dark with a desire to stand for peace and to minister as a Jesuit in the Catholic Church.

The experience turned out to be deeply spiritual, prayerful and peaceful, and empowered me not only to continue my journey into Gospel peacemaking, but to trust more and more in the invitation of God's Spirit, no matter how great the personal risk or loss of security might be. In the end, I was not dismissed from the Jesuit community, but invited to profess perpetual vows as a Jesuit. The experience taught me the power of nonviolence when engaged in the spirit of risky love. Such a loving power could not only transform the Pentagon, the Society of Jesus, the Roman Catholic Church, but even my own heart.

In preparing for sacramental civil disobedience, we must open ourselves to the providence of God, despite great risks, in the hope that our nonviolence, if pure and loving enough, might be a means to transform the hearts of many. If we are willing to risk our very lives in active nonviolence, we must expect the worst suffering, persecution, insecurity, marginalization, imprisonment, and possibly death; but we must also seek to spark a lightning fire of nonviolence that can help expose and transform the injustice we oppose.

In our preparations, we must look at every possible outcome, be prepared for the worst, but hope for the best, and have such a deep faith in the power of God's love that we expect the miracle of transformation to occur through us and our witness. We must be prepared for a violent response from the police. We must learn the lesson of Kent State* and be prepared to be shot at. This means that we must be prepared to respond deeply with nonviolent, forgiving love. Then we will discover whether our nonviolent civil disobedience was sacramental or not.

---

* On May 4th, 1970, four unarmed Kent State University students were killed (and nine more wounded) by the Ohio National Guard, during a peace rally opposing the expansion of the Vietnam War into Cambodia.

The task at hand requires a steadfast commitment to nonviolence, a constant focus on God as well as a Buddhist detachment from results. In his book, *Seeking the Face of God*, William Shannon describes three stages of Gandhian nonviolence which we can apply to the expectations we have regarding our nonviolent civil disobedience. First, we must be committed to *ahimsa*, the Sanskrit word for "noninjury", which Gandhi translates as nonviolence or unconditional love for people.

Secondly, we must express a "firmness in the truth" or a "persistence in truth" which he called *satyagraha*. Gandhi translated this word as "the force that is born of truth and love." It means courageous resistance to evil through actions that are always nonviolent and loving.

Thirdly, Gandhi advocated *nishkamakarma*, attachment from results even when we risk our lives in pursuit of the results of justice and peace. Shannon explains:

> The word *karma* concerns the inevitable and inexorable effect that our every action has on us. There is no escape from the welcome or the unwelcome consequences of our minutest thoughts and actions. The only salvation from this inevitable link of consequences to actions is to perform one's actions in such a way that one lets go of attachment to the consequences of his/her actions. This is the meaning of *nishkama-karma*. Literally it means action without desire. *Nishkama-karma* detaches us, as it were, from the chain of action-reaction... *nishkama-karma* simply means that one does his/her duty (*dharma*).

Whether doing it will achieve the result of peace or conflict resolution, I cannot tell; and while I am not uninterested in the outcome, my principal motivation must be not to achieve some desired result but to embody truth and love in what I do. Once the actions, which I perform and into which I try to put truth and love get into the public forum they mingle with the actions of others (over which I may have little or no control) and their direction may be changed. They may not be able to achieve the end I might have hoped for when I performed them. Though they seem to fail, I must still do the truth and the loving thing. This is the meaning of *nishkama-karma*: I do what I must do regardless of the results.[1]

"*Nishkama-karma* requires that I let go of the fruits of what I do," Shannon notes, "so that my acts may truly be in the service of truth and love." This must be our disposition if we want our civil disobedience to be sacramental.

In our desire to do God's will, and our fidelity in doing God's will, we will undoubtedly have to risk our very lives and walk in darkness, as Jesus did. Martin Luther King Jr.'s decision to risk arrest in Birmingham on Good Friday in 1963 is an excellent example of a risky act of nonviolence. It was an act taken in faith, with no certainty about the outcome; a moment of truth, discerned in prayer, and enacted sacramentally, that witnessed to the peace of Christ and bore the fruit of peace.

To the chagrin of other activists, he and Ralph Abernathy broke a court injunction against leading demonstrations, by walking through downtown Birmingham to a park and kneeling in prayer. King had been responsible for raising the bail money for hundreds of young people still in jail for their protest, and by this time, several weeks into the campaign, they had used up all their funds. If King risked arrest, it could bring the entire Birmingham campaign to a halt.

At a meeting on the morning of Good Friday, King's aides analyzed the financial crisis and a sense of hopelessness came upon them all. They pleaded with King not to do the action, but to keep raising money. "Martin, you can't go to jail," someone argued. "We need money. We need a lot of money. You are the only one who has the contacts to get it. If you go to jail, we are lost. The battle of Birmingham is lost." In his book, Let the Trumpet Sound, biographer Stephen Oates describes what followed next:

King was in agony. The man was right. Yet [King] had announced to Birmingham and to all the country that he was going to get arrested today. How could he face his people if he broke his promise? What would his critics say what would the country think if he now refused to go to jail after urging hundreds [in the black community] to make jail their badge of honor?

"I sat in the midst of the deepest quiet I have ever felt," King said later. Then he rose and went into a bedroom at the back of the [hotel] suite. And he stood there in the middle of the room and the center of "all that my life had brought me to be."

There was no choice really. He had to make his witness, on the faith that God would not abandon him in this dismal hour. With that faith, he changed into his work clothes, blue jeans and a blue cotton shirt and returned to the group in the next room. "I'm going to jail," he said. "I don't know what will happen. I don't know where the money will come from. But I have to make a faith act." Though there was muttering among his lieutenants, King had them join hands and sing *We Shall Overcome*.[2]

That afternoon, after a brief prayer service, King and Abernathy processed downtown until they came face to face with police chief Bull Connor, who was shouting directly at them. They knelt down, were immediately arrested and taken off to jail. King was put in solitary confinement until the next afternoon, when President Kennedy ordered the Birmingham police to take better care of him.

"Those were the longest, most frustrating hours I have lived," King said later. He described himself as being "in a nightmare of despair" about the movement.

By Easter Sunday, conditions had improved and on Monday, a lawyer friend arrived from New York with the news that over fifty thousand dollars had been raised over the weekend to pay the bail for those still left behind bars. "I cannot express what I felt," King told an audience later, "but I knew at that moment that God's presence had never left me, that God had been with me there in solitary."

In the remaining days, King penned his *Letter from a Birmingham Jail*, the manifesto of the civil rights movement, a declaration of the ideals of nonviolent resistance to injustice. King inspired Birmingham's black women, men and children to demonstrate until their demands were met. The entire nation was galvanized by the steadfast nonviolent resistance of the protesters, who withstood fire hoses and police dogs to state their case. In a short time, their immediate goals were realized. More importantly, they called the nation and the world to make justice a reality.

Sacramental civil disobedience requires that we cultivate a spirit of gratitude and love as we go forth in our public witness. We must accept the consequences of our witness of nonviolence in civil disobedience as a blessing and a gift from God. In itself, the witness will then be a revelation of God's love and truth expressed concretely in the public arena through human beings to transform the world.

In such a spirit, we can accept whatever happens and use it as an opportunity to speak the truth and call for the conversion of our society. In this spirit, we can be at peace, knowing that whatever happens, God can use us to do God's will to bring forth God's reign among us. Whatever happens, we need not be afraid, for God will be with us in the sacrament. Our civil disobedience will bear the good fruit of peace.

NINE

Testifying to the Truth

Sacramental witness in court

The synoptic Gospels record that when Jesus approached Jerusalem and prepared for his act of nonviolent civil disobedience at the Temple and the probable consequences of arrest, jail, trial and execution that would follow, he told his disciples that the courtroom would be the place where they would be able to proclaim the truth of God's reign. Mark's Gospel, the earliest of the four, advises Christians, in the words of Jesus, to speak boldly when dragged into court, for the Spirit of God will be present:

> Watch out for yourselves. They will hand you over to the courts. You will be beaten in synagogues. You will be arraigned before governors and kings because of me, as a witness before them. But the gospel must first be preached to all nations. When they lead you away and hand you over, do not worry beforehand about what you are to say. But say whatever will be given to you at that hour. For it will not be you who are speaking but the holy spirit" (Mark 13:9-11).

Luke's Gospel gives a similar message: "I myself shall give you a wisdom in speaking that all your adversaries will be powerless to resist or refute," Jesus tells them (Luke 21:15). Matthew's Gospel includes the same admonition: "Do not worry about how you are to speak, or what you are to say... the Spirit of your God [will be] speaking through you" (Mt. 10:19-20).

Unless the charges against us for our nonviolent civil disobedience are dropped, we will inevitably face arraignment hearings in a courtroom to plead our case before a judge. We may even have the opportunity of going to trial before a judge or jury because of our action. These moments in court can be sacred opportunities. According to the Gospels, they can be sacramental: special times when God is present to speak the truth through human beings about God's plan of justice and salvation.

Following these Gospel admonitions and the example of Jesus himself, we can use the courtroom as an opportunity to testify in public to the reasons for our peacemaking, our faith in God and our nonviolent resistance to evil. Court proceedings provide a chance to proclaim our allegiance to God and God's reign and our obedience to God's higher laws of justice and nonviolent love.

During Jesus' own trial, he testified to the truth of his life. The Gospel of Luke notes that Jesus had been charged with inciting the people to revolt, urging them not to pay taxes, and claiming to be the Messiah. According to the Gospel of John, Jesus spoke boldly from his heart about his own vocation as he stood before Pilate.

When Pilate asked him, "What have you done?" Jesus replied: "My kingdom does not belong to this world. If my kingdom did belong to this world, my attendants would be fighting to keep me from being handed over to the Jews. But as it is, my kingdom is not here... You say I am a king. For this I was born and for this I came into the world, to testify to the truth. Everyone who belongs to the truth listens to my voice" (John 18:33-37).

In a nutshell, Jesus explained the difference between the reign of God and the kingdoms and empires of this world, a difference rooted in nonviolence. He clarified his whole life's work before Pilate, by defining his mission to speak the truth.

Today, the courtroom provides us with a setting to speak boldly and publicly to the nation about the injustices that plague the world, the root causes of these injustices in our own system, and the urgent need to eradicate these evils. During the twentieth century, perhaps the most dramatic use of the courtroom for charges of civil disobedience was Gandhi's appearance before a British judge on March 18, 1922, in Ahmedabad, India.

Gandhi was charged with sedition and disturbing the peace. When asked if he wished to make a statement, Gandhi stood up and said he would save the prosecution the time and energy of trying to prove whether or not he was guilty of opposing British rule. He continued:

It is very true and I have no desire whatsoever to conceal from this court the fact that to preach disaffection toward the existing system of government has become almost a passion with me. Indeed, [I] have preached sedition long before the prosecutor said I had. I do not ask for mercy. I do not plead any extenuating act. I am here therefore, to invite and cheerfully submit to the highest penalty that can be inflicted upon me for what in law is a deliberate crime and what appears to me to be the highest duty of a citizen.

The only course open to you, the Judge, is, as I am going to say in my statement, either to resign your post, or inflict on me the severest penalty if you believe that the system and the law you administer are good for the people. I do not expect that kind of conversion, but by the time I have finished with my statement you will perhaps have a glimpse of what is raging within my breast to run this maddest risk that a person can run. In my opinion, non-cooperation with evil is as much a duty as is cooperation with good.[1]

After praising Gandhi for his high ideals and "saintly life," the judge sentenced him to six years imprisonment. Gandhi went off to prison with a smile. His statement and the judge's sentence stirred the hearts of millions of Indians who recommitted themselves to the movement for independence from Britain.

Though he went to jail many times during the next twenty-five years of his life, Gandhi was never tried or arraigned again in court because of the British government's fear of the power of his public testimony.

For Christians engaged in sacramental civil disobedience, the court proceedings that we face give us an opportunity to witness in the Spirit of God to the truth of our faith lives and the truth of nonviolence which we have learned from the Gospels. Court proceedings offer a public stage from which we can speak the truth about the injustices and systemic violence that plague our world and the need for the world to be transformed into a haven of justice and nonviolent love. These court hearings can be occasions to invite people into the new life of Christian faith, and the nonviolent struggle for justice and peace that adherence to God's reign entails.

As we plead guilty or not guilty and explain our actions before a judge or a jury, we can articulate the vision of justice and peace that lies at the heart of our obedience to God in God's reign. We can use the language of the court to explain this vision, by speaking about international law, the principles of human rights, and the traditions of our society which uphold freedom and justice. We can appeal to human decency, morality, and the values behind the law, and then point to the law of God as the highest law of the land, the law which governs the human race.

In the attempt to explain our adherence to God's law, we can announce the basic tenets of the biblical covenant which humans are invited to keep with God: "Do not worship false gods or idols. Do not kill. Do not commit injustice. Do not wage war against anyone. Love one another. Love your enemies. Practice nonviolent justice towards the poor. Be compassionate as God is compassionate. Let the one without sin be the first to throw a stone."

By transforming the court proceedings with such proclamations and appeals, we can speak not only to the conscience of the judge and the jury, but through them, to the conscience of the nation. We appeal to their consciences, to the love and goodness in their hearts. We can invoke the use of civil disobedience in the noble movements of history that have abolished slavery, secured the right of women to vote, and established basic civil rights for African-Americans all in the effort to explain our action and the reason why we resorted to nonviolent civil disobedience. We hope we will so move our hearers that they will take new action and promote God's reign.

We are not concerned with winning or losing

Ultimately, we do not enter the court proceedings to nit-pick over the legalities regarding our civil disobedience. It may be helpful to ask for "discovery" of police reports and other evidence, to think through our opening and closing statements and the cross examination of witnesses, and to be aware of one's legal rights in the courtroom; but if we focus solely on legal rules and jargon, we may miss an opportunity to touch the hearts of those present and all those who will hear of our witness.

By avoiding legal intricacies, speaking from the heart about our action and our faith, and focusing on our obedience to God's higher laws of justice and peace, we can continue the sacrament of civil disobedience and once again help touch the hearts of others. We want to continue to proclaim God's truth of justice and peace in the loving presence of the Spirit, no matter where we are, and the courtroom is an official forum in the world for us to speak about our citizenship in God's reign.

We are not so much concerned with winning or losing as in reaching out to our fellow human beings with the good news of Jesus. "I never saw the trials as trying to turn the system to our advantage," Daniel Berrigan once said in an interview, referring to his many trials for civil disobedience. In the case of the Plowshares Eight, some of the group were reticent to cooperate with the trial at all, believing the process to be corrupted or invalid.

"I argued very strongly that we must tell our story," Daniel explained. "We don't owe anything to the court; we owe it to the people supporting us, to the people of the country, to everybody. It's part of our vocation to explain our actions."

> So I would ask Phil and the others things like, Who's going to come to a trial where nothing's happening? What's it going to mean to people? What's it going to mean to the media? Are we interested in communicating why we did this action? Then we have to go into court and say our thing. But that's the only reason we cooperated. None of us expected to win or be acquitted or whatever.[2]

We must keep in mind that the US judicial and legal system and that of other countries is not rooted in God's way of nonviolence and love, but in the system of punishment that defends the privileged and powerful, indeed, the system itself.

Justification defenses or biblically-rooted critiques that permit activists to explain the legality, morality and necessity of their nonviolent witness because of the crisis in the culture, are rarely allowed in courtrooms today.[3] The facts of the nuclear arsenal and systemic injustice or the imminence of the climate catastrophe are usually not permitted as evidence.

Personal testimonies, however, usually are allowed, though judges may instruct the juries to disregard the motives behind our civil disobedience. Though jurors rarely know it, they can, in turn, disregard a judge's instructions and act independently to make a decision in accord with their conscience. Unfortunately, juries are too often intimidated and fail to grasp the power they have to reach a dramatic verdict that would convict the unjust system itself.

We therefore cannot expect justice in a courtroom; or at least, that should not be our main concern. As we speak in the courtroom, we should recall and return to the original spirit which moved us to commit the nonviolent civil disobedience in the first place. In that spirit of God's love and truth, we will reach out to others including the judge, the lawyers and the jury and invite them to the truth of God's Way of peace. We must seek justice from God's perspective for all human beings, and thus be detached from the expectation of finding justice before a judge in a human court.

The court gives us a platform to speak about the realities of injustice. These words may enlighten the minds and touch the hearts of all who hear them, and in that moment, the reign of God will be proclaimed. This is the task before us as we go to court for our nonviolent civil disobedience. It is enough, then, to trust in the presence of the Holy Spirit, which Jesus promised, and to remain faithful and consistent in our witness. The Holy Spirit of God will handle the rest.

Daniel Berrigan's testimony

The testimony of Daniel Berrigan at the first Plowshares Eight trial in Norristown, Pennsylvania in March, 1981, and his subsequent testimony at a final appeal hearing in April, 1990, demonstrate the dramatic possibilities of proclaiming the good news of peace in the public forum of a US courtroom. At the original Plowshares Eight Trial, Dan Berrigan spoke about the influence of his parents and community, and the religious convictions that undergird his nonviolent actions. I include it at length here:

Dear friends of the jury, you have been called the conscience of the community. Each of us eight comes from a community. I don't mean just a biological family. I mean that every one of us has brothers and sisters with whom we live, with whom we pray, with whom we offer the Eucharist, with whom we share income, and in some cases, the care of children. Our conscience, in other words, comes from somewhere. We have not come from outer space or from chaos or from madhouses to [the G.E. plant in] King of Prussia [Pennsylvania].

I am trying to say that we come, as a community of conscience, before *your* community of conscience to ask you: Are our consciences to act differently than yours, in regard to the lives and deaths of children? We would like you to see that we come from where you come from. We come from churches. We come from neighborhoods. We come from years of work. We come from America. And we come to this, a trial, of conscience and motive.

And the statement of conscience we would like to present to you is this: We could not *not* do this. We could not *not* do this! We were pushed to this by all our lives. Do you see what I mean? All our lives... With every cowardly bone in my body I wished I hadn't had to enter the GE plant. I wish l hadn't had to do it. And that has been true every time l have been arrested, all those years.

My stomach turns over. I feel sick. I feel afraid. I don't want to go through this again. I hate jail. I don't do well there physically. But I cannot *not* go on, because I have learned that we must not kill if we are Christians. I have learned that children, above all, are threatened by these weapons. I have read that Christ our Lord underwent death rather than inflict it. And l am supposed to be a disciple. All kinds of things like that. The push of conscience is a terrible thing.

We believe, according to the law the law of the state of Pennsylvania, that we were justified in saying, "We cannot live with [nuclear weapons]"; justified in saying it publicly, saying it dramatically, saying it with blood and hammers; because that weapon, and the hundreds and hundreds more being produced in our country, are the greatest evil conceivable on this earth.

There is no evil to compare with that. Multiply murder. Multiply desolation. The mind boggles. So we went into that death factory, and in a modest, self-contained, careful way, we put a few dents in two missiles, awaited arrest, came willingly into court to talk to you. We believe with all our hearts that our action was justified.[4]

In explaining his action and sharing his personal fears and hopes in such a reasonable and poetic manner, Berrigan touched a nerve in the broader community. He used the courtroom to explain publicly the truth that he and his friends have come upon in their own lives: that faith in God and concern for human beings requires nonviolent opposition to nuclear weapons.

Berrigan continued:

We have spent years and years of our adult lives keeping the law. We have tried everything, every access, every means to get to public authorities within the law. We come from within the law, from within. We are deeply respectful of a law that is in favor of human life. And as we know, at least some of our laws are. We are very respectful of those laws. We want you to know that.

Years and years we spent writing letters, trying to talk to authorities, vigiling in public places, holding candles at night, holding placards by day, trying, trying, fasting, trying to clarify things to ourselves as were trying to speak to others; all of that within the law, years of it.

And then I had to say, I could not *not* break the law and remain human. If we kept forever on this side of the line, we would die within, ourselves. We couldn't look in the mirror, couldn't face those we love, had no Christian message in the world, nothing to say if we went on that way.

Our act is all I have to say. The only message I have to the world is: We are not allowed to kill innocent people. We are not allowed to be complicit in murder. We are not allowed to be silent while preparations for mass murder proceed in our name, with our money, secretly Thou shall not kill; we are not allowed to kill. Everything today comes down to that—everything.[5]

Berrigan's testimony reached a climax with this plea of truth: *Thou shalt not kill.* It was an appeal not only to the judge and the jury, but to the church and the nation itself. This plea for conversion was at the heart of his whole statement. "If the Plowshares Eight have insisted on anything," Berrigan later wrote, "it is that their trial and imprisonment are not the issue at stake. Pity for them gains nothing. Neither does fear for them or for their children and spouses. [The issue] is the corporate crimes of General Electric [and] the race toward oblivion."[6]

Later, in Holy Week April, 1990, at the final appeal hearing for the Plowshares Eight in a Norristown, Pennsylvania courthouse, Daniel Berrigan again spoke on behalf of the defendants. He began by referring to all those who stand for justice and peace—for example, the other Plowshares activists in jail, Nelson Mandela, Vaclav Havel who had been "named and nailed" by the court.

Then, he turned to Jesus:

One thinks inevitably this week [Holy Week] of another naming and nailing. It occurred (in a court very like this) in the first century of our era. The accused was hauled in; successive judges hurled abuse at him, as did the tempestuous crowd. He was named repeatedly, scornfully, by the Roman state and its satellite religionists and thugs: would-be destroyer of temple property, withholder of tribute money, blasphemer, pretender to a lost throne.

The charges were as sharp as nails. The names attached to him held firm. He was convicted and capitally punished. And yet, and yet. Even though the law has claimed so often to speak the last word about the accused, to name the final name, to drive the nails deep, yet some event down the road of time, an intervention, a change of heart, keeps intruding. A seismic shift occurs in consciences.

We hear a later, far different word attaching itself to Mandela, Havel, Sakharov, Jesus, and countless other noble criminals, whether in our lifetime or long before.

No court, in fact, seems able to speak a last word, or to drive a final nail, even in a coffin. The scornful names fall to rot in the rude weathers of time; the nails rust and spring apart.

Which is to say, justice in contrast to the law tends to get heard eventually, to forge new names on behalf of the vilified, to raise the very dead... Let it only be said that the sentences meted out today...are in better hands than ours, or our judges'. In the hands, let us pray, of a Holy Defendant once reviled and misnamed in an earthly court, named and finally nailed in infamy. His wounds, we believe, are healed and glorious.

And his name is above every name, every earthly power and dominion. Including the power and dominion of this court, or of any court of history. It is to him, finally, we proffer our argument. The argument goes this way. If the children of the world are accounted safer for our being imprisoned, so be it. We go in a good spirit. If the Earth will be freer of its nuclear illness and insult for our being imprisoned, so be it. We go in a good spirit. If first-strike weaponry is to be judged within the law, and we outside the law, so be it. We go to prison in a good spirit.[7]

Berrigan and the Plowshares activists trusted in the Holy Spirit, and spoke the truth as they saw it. Berrigan's words and the words of his friends were inspiring to everyone. Afterwards, the prosecutor declared that the defendants had offered "compelling and eloquent testimony," and the judge admitted that he too was impressed. He confessed that he had intended to send them off to years in prison, but instead, sentenced them to time served. The message, proclaimed in court, gave hope that hearts can be moved.

The liberation of testimony

The courtroom is the place for public testimony to the truth of the Gospel. It is the place for Christians who witness to the Way of nonviolence and justice to stand up and side publicly with Jesus and his vision of a new world order. The courtroom is a place where the Spirit can be unleashed to address the evils of systemic injustice and institutionalized violence. It is the place where activists can stand up and tell truth to power about the realities of the climate crisis. It may not lead to concrete changes, but it can pave the way for the transformation of the public consciousness about issues of justice and injustice.

I have experienced the spiritual potential of publicly testifying to the truth in many courtrooms up and down the East and West coasts for my own acts of nonviolent civil disobedience. After my first arrest for sitting-in at the Pentagon, for example, I was ordered to appear before a magistrate in Alexandria, Virginia. I pleaded not guilty to the charge of trespassing, and was then allowed to explain the reasons for my action.

During my testimony, I told of my discipleship to the peacemaking Jesus and the urgent need to abolish our nuclear weapons and for all of us to become a people of nonviolence. I also testified to God's higher law of mercy and justice, a law, I concluded, which was rooted not in the nuclear violence of the Pentagon but in the nonviolence of the Sermon on the Mount, a law which we must all adhere to. The magistrate thanked me for my reflections and praised my idealism, but concluded that the "law is the law," that I had broken it, and therefore that I was guilty as charged.

Though I may not have changed anyone's mind about the work of the Pentagon, and though the magistrate did not have a conversion towards God's way of disarmament, he did suspend my sentence, and I felt empowered to go forth and speak the truth about the Gospel as never before.

The opportunity to testify to the truth in court was a deep experience of liberation, for I felt freer now to live out publicly my discipleship to Jesus. Before that first court hearing, I was still somewhat intimidated, inhibited and afraid of my stand for justice and peace; but afterwards, I felt emboldened in the Spirit.

Testifying in a courtroom can be an experience of liberation. The Spirit within us is set free publicly to touch the hearts and minds of others, and in that process, we are empowered to take greater risks and bolder stands for God's truth of love and justice for the poor. We become even more shameless in our passion for the reign of God.

In October 1988 I, along with six friends who worked with the homeless and advocated low-income housing, staged a mock eviction on a street in front of the US Capitol in Washington, DC. We unloaded couches, chairs, lamps, and other furniture in the middle of the street to dramatize the plight of the homeless poor in the nation's capitol and across the country. We were arrested, jailed and arraigned and our case came to trial in January, 1989.

For three days, we testified about the realities of homelessness in the United States. Though the prosecution tried to limit our defense to the strict charge of blocking a street, we convinced the judge of our right to appeal to a higher moral law in our defense, and were able to explain how our action was necessary to call Congress' attention to the plight of the homeless poor.

Several of us acted as our own lawyers, and found the experience of making opening and closing arguments, as well as testifying on the witness stand, a powerful way to speak the truth about justice for the poor. Before a packed courtroom, the jury found us not guilty and the judge openly wept and asked for our prayers. It was an experience that empowered us and touched the hearts of all those who were present.

The courtroom is a place to let the light of truth shine publicly. This setting provides the context for ordinary Christians to speak prophetically and to proclaim the truth in the tradition of modern-day prophets of peace, such as Martin Luther King Jr., Oscar Romero and Dorothy Day. Our message in the courtroom can be like the prophetic word offered by Archbishop Romero to the soldiers of the Salvadoran military on March 23, 1980, a message which resulted in his assassination the following day:

"Brothers, you are part of our own people. You kill your own campesino brothers and sisters. And before an order that a man may give to kill, God's law must prevail: Thou shalt not kill! No soldier is obliged to obey an order against the law of God. No one has to fulfill an immoral law. It is time to take back your consciences and to obey your consciences rather than the orders of sin. The church, defender of the rights of God, of the law of God, of human dignity, of the person, cannot remain silent before such abominations.[8]

The public, political message of Allan Boesak of South Africa is another example of the kind of testimony that we can proclaim in our own courtrooms regarding the evils within our own systems. When the pro-apartheid South African president warned the churches to "toe the government line" in March, 1988, Boesak replied in a homily that the mission of the church was to "toe only God's line":

[The president] says [to the church], "Speak to the Christian message." Well, Mr. Minister, let me say again if you had read the Gospels, if your church had taught you, you would not have spoken such utter nonsense.

To feed the poor and clothe the naked is the Christian message. To fight for justice is the Christian message. To say that peace without justice is impossible in South Africa, as anywhere else in the world, is the Christian message. To say that a government which knows no justice, and denies God, is illegitimate and will die ignominiously is the Christian message.

To proclaim to this government, that in your denial of the word of God, in your insistence upon oppression, in your persecution of the church of Jesus Christ, you have ceased to become the servant of God of Romans 13—but have become the beast from the sea of Revelation 13—that is the Christian message that the government must hear.

To call upon God's people to obey God, rather than the government, is the Christian message. Amidst all of the warnings that we get these days, we have to proclaim one thing, and this is that Jesus Christ is Lord. I know how difficult it sometimes may be. I know how I felt on that Thursday night when that brick flew through our window—fortunately without hurting any of our children.

But it must be said: Jesus Christ is Lord. I want to say this as calmly as I possibly can. Mr. Minister, you can threaten us all you like. Jesus Christ is Lord. Let your security police terrorize our children and threaten our lives. Jesus Christ is Lord. You can come into the streets and into our churches and you can massacre us. Jesus Christ is Lord. The battle is on! But Jesus Christ is Lord... No government can challenge the living God and survive.[9]

Our mission is to proclaim as bold a message as possible—one that will not harden the hearts of the judge, the jury or our fellow citizens, but move them, invite them to conversion and challenge them to take action for justice and peace. Our appeal must be pure, simple and convincing. If we come from a consistent lifestyle of integrity, peacemaking, gentleness and love for the poor, our opposition to the evils of the age will be all the more compelling.

In Germany, nonviolent resisters have been so eloquent and convincing in the courtroom that judges have begun to join the anti-nuclear movement. A coalition of over eight hundred judges and prosecutors have marched for peace, sat-in at US military bases, and handed down minimal sentences to anti-nuclear defendants.[10] The possibility of such a human response by those in authority reminds us to withhold a self-righteous, judgmental attitude towards judges or other officials. In order to be consistent with our ethic and lifestyle of nonviolence, we must remain loving towards all the human beings we meet, even in the courtrooms and the prisons to which we are sentenced.

Because of that love, conversion of heart and the transformation of systemic injustice *can* begin to happen. Mary Lou Kownacki challenged those in the peace movement to be aware of our own sinful habit of judging others, particularly judges, when she shared a recent experience in the courtroom where "distrust, and even disdain, for the supposed opponent seemed present."

Kownacki felt personal empathy for the judge—who seemed genuinely caught between the pressures of the law, and his personal sympathy for the position of the defendants. The judge confessed to be "agonizing" over the case, "the most difficult of my career"—and Kownacki believed him. Others were not so empathetic:

To read an account of the proceedings in a movement newsletter made me wonder if l had been in the same courtroom; so negative, so smug and self-righteous was its interpretation of the judge's motives, words and actions. He was not treated as a person, but as an "enemy."[11]

If we maintain the spirit of peace and love that shows no animosity towards anyone, the judge, the prosecutor, the jury, the police officers and others who are called to testify against us, we will present a clearer statement for peace and justice. Our prayerfulness will insure a pure witness of love and speed up the answer to our prayers.

When we find ourselves in a courtroom before a judge, we can maintain a spirit of deep respect and love for the judge and other officials, like Gandhi, and still gratefully decline any offer of paying a fine or doing community service. We can cling to the truth in a deep spirit of nonviolence and trust in the integrity of that truth. That spirit of love and truth will make our opposition to war and systemic injustice of all kinds all the more powerful, until the truth of our witness becomes irresistible, and judges the world over refuse to try nonviolent anti-war, anti-injustice, ecological activists.

In this spirit of love, we can stand in courtrooms all over the world, testifying about our nonviolent actions to proclaim the reality that all human beings are, in truth, citizens of God's reign; and thus, that we are all called to make justice and peace a reality on earth. Like Jesus and Gandhi, we can respectfully and lovingly withdraw our obedience to the system which defends nuclear weapons, injustice, and the abandonment of the planet.

We can insist on the truth of justice and peace, and we can do that without giving in to violence or a disrespectful attitude. We can accept the suffering meted out to us with open, loving hearts, and go to prison in a good spirit. This sacramental attitude has the power to transform our hearts and our world. The courtroom can become a place where God's transforming presence is made manifest once again, to the greater glory of God, the service of the poor, the liberation of the oppressed and the care of God's planet.

This sacramental spirit will be ultimately tested when we are sent to prison. In the prison cell, the nonviolent resister who is rooted in the love of God and who enacted civil disobedience in a sacramental spirit has the potential to spark the conscience of the nation from which the resister comes and the whole world. The power of that witness, then, is what we must finally turn to next.

TEN

Imprisoned for Sacramental Peacemaking

Learning from the witness of others

If we want our actions, our civil disobedience, and our very lives to be sacramental, we must be rooted from beginning to end in the unconditional love of God. Our civil disobedience must be the fruit of our unending life experiments in nonviolence. They must be the fruit of us plumbing the depths of God's unconditional love, which is available to each one of us in our own hearts.

In our pursuit of justice, and the proclamation of the truth, the acceptance of suffering is essential to nonviolence. One place to test our growth in unconditional love is in prison for our peacemaking activities. Prison is a place where our spiritual roots will be tested, and blossom; where suffering, accepted for justice's sake, can be lived to the fullest; where our nonviolence can come full circle as we dwell in the peace of God among the poor. It is a place where the unconditional love in our hearts, and the prayerful nonviolence of our entire lives, can bear fruit through our peaceful contemplation. Our silent presence can remind the world about the basic issues of justice and peace.

This is not to say that jail or prison life is easy; quite the contrary. "You go to jail because you have to, not because you want to," Daniel Berrigan once told an interviewer.[1] But once we are in jail, we can continue the sacramental witness of nonviolence. We can still speak out about the issues of justice and peace, through our prayers, love and outreach.

The loving witness of a nonviolent resister who taps into the love of God can be a spiritual explosion of love in the world. It touches the hearts of many, and leads to the transformation of the unjust structures of our world. On the personal level, it can be a concrete spiritual experience of joy and peace in the midst of suffering; on the public level, it can offer a tremendous witness of nonviolence, conscience and integrity to the world. It can be a participation in God's redemptive, transforming love, calling everyone to God's own peace and justice.

Prison as an experience of disarmament and resurrection

After an act of civil disobedience towards systemic injustice, entering prison with a spirit of nonviolent love can be a way to liberation: a way to take up one's cross and enter into the depths of the resurrection. So wrote activist and theologian Jim Douglass:

"When brothers and sisters resist the powers of
domination with love and with truth, their lives
celebrate life with a passion which scandalizes the
joyless holders of power: Why are they so happy? Won't
someone please tell them it's a jail, that they don't have
the keys and can't get out? Why don't they understand
that they can't be that happy?"[2]

The purpose of prisons, Douglass observes, is "raw power
in the service of a ruling class." The task of the nonviolent
resister is not to fight power with greater power, i.e., greater
violence, but to fight the power of systemic violence by
letting go of all power, and entering into the powerlessness
of nonviolence.

This incarnated nonviolence, within the context of
prison, can make our very lives sacramental; a living
prayer. Douglass calls it "an act of Being"; it is "technically
ineffective, [but] spiritually explosive." By rejecting the
very idea of "effectiveness", prison's threat of force and
confinement is nullified from the start:

If my choice of prison through resistance is to be
sustained in me, as it has been in others, I must
renounce all ends from the beginning (what end can
be served by my silence behind bars?) and give myself
fully to the silence of a way which offers no guarantees
for truth and love... Prison, like death on a cross, can in
faith open a way into a valley of silence where life flows
without ceasing."[3]

"One way of seeing jail today," Douglass concludes, "is to regard it as the new monastery. In a society preparing for nuclear war and ignoring its poor, jail is an appropriate setting in which to give one's life to prayer. In a nation that has legalized preparations for the destruction of all life on earth, going to jail—through nonviolent civil disobedience—can be seen as a prayer. In reflecting today on the Lord's prayer, I think that going to jail as a way of saying *thy kingdom come, thy will be done'* may be the most basic prayer we can offer in the 'nuclear security state'."

Douglass explains that his deepest experiences of peace occurred in "the two most violent places I've ever been": the Strategic Weapons Facility Pacific (SWFPAC), where he prayed for peace and forgiveness next to huge concrete bunkers; and LA County jail, "where people are stored." The reign of God, he posits, "is realized [in such places]... I believe that a suffering God continually calls us to be [there] for the sake of peace and justice."[4]

Jail brings a strong realization that one is not in control of one's life; it takes away "the illusion that our lives are our own rather than God's," Douglass observes. There, we share life with the poor, in whom God lives. We face the reality of a God who is "at one with the oppressed":

Jail serves the same purpose today for peacemakers as the desert did for early Christian contemplatives—to overcome claims of privilege and to crack open the illusions of self-reliance and ego. I believe going to jail for peace can deepen a life of prayer in a way few monasteries can.[5]

"Most obvious at first is the helplessness, the loss of control," plowshares activist Anne Montgomery wrote from prison; "the reinforcement of all that is degrading to human dignity and self-respect." We may carry in with us a sense of peace, even exuberance, following our recent act of resistance; but on entering prison, things quickly change, as the experience transforms into that of any criminal.

Worse, she adds, is the fact that most inmates are *not* there for their conscientious resistance, but as the latest in a long line of societal rejections, having received little help or sympathy for problems borne of drugs, economic need, or abuse. It is an illusion-shattering reality:

> We who can never lose the privilege of our education, inner resources, or the free act that landed us in prison in the first place can still become more grounded in reality by touching the lives of so many unfortunate sisters and brothers, by experiencing something of their inability to choose the next meal or to find a measure of silence and solitude, something seemingly so essential to contemplation...Life in prison is part of a continuing "experiment in truth."[6]

"Just as crossing the line in action clarifies one's vision," she concludes, "so the experience of the nonaction, the seemingly useless life of prison, reveals a level of truth-force difficult to perceive from the outside." It is an opportunity to "meet violence [both] in its petty, institutionalized forms [and] in our own reactions" and "allow the transforming power of love to work in and around us" both times.

While in a Connecticut prison, Plowshares activist Judith Beaumont and her co-resisters organized a campaign to change some of the worst practices there. Her outreach to the other women prisoners, and protest of the conditions, helped lead to several reforms in the prison. "Prison can be a time to live and work with those people who are the victims of the arms race," she observes.

Philip Berrigan and Elizabeth McAlister have written that such a place offers "time to pursue the disarming of our own spirits." The barriers between the jailers and the jailed, which the state maintains at all costs, must be transcended, they write. This transformation can only happen when "the roots of one's freedom are interior" and "we cling to the common humanity between us with a limitless love."

Imprisonment for Gospel peacemaking is an experiment in poverty, loneliness, fear, displacement, systemic violence, and the grief and brokenness of other prisoners. It is a time to delve deeply into one's own violence and nonviolence, into faith, hope and love, and to accept the purification, powerlessness and uselessness of prison so that one can serve others. Prison then becomes an experience of *disarmament*, and ultimately, a mystical experience of freedom found in the incarnation of nonviolence. "In love's light, we can learn about ourselves, and how far we have to travel to be disarmed people," Berrigan and McAlister conclude.[7]

"When women in prison [for peacemaking activity], far from families and loved ones, can laugh and play, they practice resurrection," wrote Elizabeth McAlister after twenty-five months in Alderson prison for her part in the

Griffiss plowshares action.[8] Ultimately, the experience of prison as the consequence and continuation of nonviolence, as McAlister observes, is an experience of resurrection.

In January, 1991, just prior to the Persian Gulf War, Bill Frankel-Streit hammered on a B-52 bomber at Griffiss Air Force Base in New York—as part of a Plowshares action. After several weeks in jail, including two weeks in solitary confinement, he wrote about his experiences, making clear again the connections between nonviolence, peacemaking, imprisonment, contemplation and resurrection:

> This whole journey has been "graced" in a big way. I've never felt freer and more harmonious in my life. As I told the Judge, when offered release, in times of war, there is no other place, in conscience, that I could be.

> It's been a mystical type of experience: rejoicing and weeping somehow in a yin/yang Zen equation. The reading from Paul a couple of Sundays ago says it well: "Those who weep should live as though they were not weeping, and those who rejoice as though they were not rejoicing." I've found myself easily weeping over the killing in the Middle East and the killing of conscience here with blind patriotism and a cheerleading, censored media.

> But the rejoicing is immense. The Spirit has been so gracious to us from the moment we stepped out of the cover of the trees in a single-hearted commitment to pick up the cross [at the nuclear weapons base], to this moment in my cell which has, with the grace of

the Spirit, become a combination hermitage and anti-war office! These four jail walls limiting my options exteriorly has had a similar yet paradoxical effect interiorly. My options interiorly have consequently been cut off and a single-minded,single-heartedness has emerged.

There's no going back—only ahead to radical discipleship to Jesus... I'm happy. Being in jail is a continuation of the action: proclaiming resurrection in "deadly force zones." I've been meditating on radical Christianity as a call to "roll away the stone" and proclaim resurrection/new life in the midst of death. With the mustard seed faith to cast mountains into the sea, we proclaim the victory—that death has no more power over us, wherever the death-vice of the empire stretches out its entangling branches of domination—this of course includes jail.

I've been following the liturgy of the hours, following a monastic schedule of sorts. We're "locked down" which means "in" at 11:00 pm till 6:00 am, when the cell doors open with a "bang" electronically. A little plastic cup of juice is offered immediately. Then I go back to my cell to pray the office of readings (patterned after the early morning Trappist vigil prayers), contemplate and savor the only quiet 45 minutes of the day. Most guys go back to bed.

Breakfast comes, which is upward-mobility for me—milk and cereal, which was seldom available at the Catholic Worker. I pray Lauds after breakfast which is followed by cleanup and "rec" where I see one of the other Plowshares activists. There's lots of interaction with the men here. Many are joining us in our anti-war vision. It's always the poor who are better able to recognize truth.[9]

"To be in jail because of one's commitment to peace, this is the closest I have come so far to a lack of complicity in the crimes of our culture," wrote Catholic Worker Jeff Dietrich from the Los Angeles County Jail where he was sentenced after demonstrating at an "Arms Bazaar."

"Neither retreat nor vacation... could ever have produced the profound contemplative experience that I have had here in jail... Here there are few distractions and the need for that relationship [with God] is deep, so immediate, so essential, there can be no question of abandoning it. It is the very breath of life. It is more essential than food, drink or companionship. No vacation, no time off, no retreat could ever impart to me such a vision of my complete dependence upon God. I have never had such a feeling of peace, fulfillment, [or] satisfaction with myself." [10]

Examples of sacramental witness from prison

It is clear enough: if we accept our time in prison in the Spirit of nonviolent love, in the same manner in which we engaged in sacramental civil disobedience, then we can experience the God of Peace in our lives. Such accepted powerlessness can unleash the power of God's transforming love in our hearts, in the prison and in the world itself. The experience of prison can then be spiritually explosive.

We are "reduced to zero," as Gandhi said; spiritually emptied like Jesus, as St. Paul wrote. We become freer to dwell in the peaceful presence of God. God uses our very hearts, souls, spirits and bodies to speak to humanity about the needs of justice and peace. We become light to the world. But as one Christian wrote from a prison in the Philippines: "To give light, one has to endure burning."

Christian peacemakers, from Paul and the early Christians to Dorothy Day and the Berrigans have understood this phenomenon of grace: people draw strength and courage from those who suffer persecution and imprisonment yet who continue to speak the truth and to keep the faith in a spirit of love. Today, the prison letters of Paul and the lives of Thoreau, Gandhi, King, Jaegerstaetter, Day, and the Berrigans, as well as countless unknown nonviolent resisters, show us the power of nonviolence to transform the world.

These nonviolent resisters did not go seeking imprisonment; but they were willing to take the peacemaking Scriptures seriously, to proclaim the good news about God's way of nonviolence, come what may. For the remainder of this chapter, I offer their stories—as seen in their writings and the biographies others have written. Their Gospel witness challenges us all to wake up and walk the risky path of nonviolent civil disobedience. They invite us to a new sacramental life. They show us that in our civil disobedience, our trials and our imprisonment, we too can meet the God of nonviolence.

The imprisonment of the early Christians

"The state has only one power it can use against human beings, and that is death," William Stringfellow once wrote. "The State can persecute you, prosecute you, imprison you, exile you, execute you. All of these ean come to the same thing. The State can consign you to death. The grace of Jesus Christ in this life is that death fails. There is nothing the State can do to you, or to me, which we need fear."[11]

The early Christians understood this radical freedom from the fear of death, discovered in discipleship to Jesus. They went from their upper room prayer services into the streets with the word of Christ's love. They were quickly rounded up, arrested and imprisoned by the imperial authorities. Many of them were tortured and killed.

Yet so many of them remained faithful to Christ. They followed Christ onto the streets with the good news; they also followed Christ to the cross, and then, in faith, into new life—the Spirit of resurrection. Because of their faithful following in the footsteps of Jesus, the good news of Jesus spread; people all over the world heard about Jesus and his Way of peace. Their active peacemaking and their peaceful acceptance of suffering, in prison and in death, touched the hearts of thousands. Their story gives evidence that the Way of Jesus—the Way of nonviolence—can indeed be redemptive and transforming.

After the crucifixion and resurrection of Jesus, as the years went on, more and more sisters and brothers were imprisoned and executed. The early community began to exhort its members to visit those in prison. Scripture passages such as Matthew 25:36 and Hebrews 13:3 may have been a particular effort of the evangelists to get community members to visit their brothers and sisters in prison. God is with those in prison, we are told. Indeed, Jesus Christ is in prison. *Go, visit Christ there*, they urged.

Between the lines, we read: go and be there yourself. Luke's gospel is the clearest on this possibility, as we have seen. In chapter 21, after lengthy discourses and lessons about the Way of nonviolent love, Jesus tells his followers that they will be imprisoned. *Agape* is not accepted in this world, he observes. The empire will try to crush all the forces of love and truth. "They will lay their hands on you and persecute you," Jesus declares, "delivering you up to the synagogues and prisons " (21:12-13).

The Book of Revelation, in particular, emerged from a Christian community of resisters who faced deadly persecution from the empire. The writer urges Christians to persevere. In effect, we are told: be faithful to Christ, who was faithful to the way of nonviolent love, even through prison, torture and assassination. "Do not fear what you are about to suffer," Revelation states. "Behold, the devil is about to throw some of you into prison, that you may be tested, and for ten days you will have tribulation. Be faithful unto death, and I will give you the crown of life. [The one] who has an ear, let them hear what the Spirit says to the churches" (Rev. 2:10-11).

The most famous early Christian, the apostle Paul, was imprisoned on numerous occasions, and wrote many of his letters from prison. In his second letter to the Corinthians, Paul bragged of his sufferings and accomplishments.*

By calling attention to his sufferings—including his imprisonments—Paul seeks the sympathy of his audience, and impresses on them the authenticity and integrity of his character. In his second letter to the Corinthians, he claims to have suffered "far more imprisonments" than the so-called super-apostles, and thus, he defends his status as "Apostle of Christ" (2 Cor. 11:22-29; 12:9-10).

Paul lists his imprisonments and sufferings to demonstrate his Gospel integrity as a follower of the crucified One—so that he can then preach the folly of the nonviolent cross and the Gospel of peace. His imprisonments allow him to boast of the power of Christ and the Gospel, to a people who were already beginning to feel the pinch of this New Life. From prison, he felt "strongest" as a disciple. He knew, as we know now, that accepting Christ, becoming a disciple of Christ and practicing *agape* would inevitably lead to a conflict with the powers of violence and death.

This reality so terrified the early community that most waited until they were near death to be baptized. In those days, baptism into discipleship of the nonviolent Christ meant certain imprisonment and death. By explaining the day to day cost of discipleship in his own life, and yet maintaining a spirit of hope and joy in the risen Jesus, Paul

---

* See p.103 (or 2 Cor. 6:5-8).

was able to give a true witness to Christ. His message was contagious. People dropped everything to sign up for this New Life. They, too, then joined the movement of Christ's peace, and risked imprisonment and martyrdom.

Paul used his imprisonment to his advantage. Philippians 1:7-21 explains that the reason for Paul's imprisonment— and thus his story about the Christ—spread through the whole praetorium.* In his faith, Paul is convinced that his imprisonment has furthered his vocation of evangelization. His notoriety has served to advance the gospel and the word about Christ. People have learned that his imprisonment is for Christ, and this becomes an underlying cause for his rejoicing.

Additionally, his imprisonment has actually strengthened other Christians, making them "confident" and "much more bold to speak the word of God without fear." For Paul, this accomplishment would be a great gift of the Spirit. It is the fruit of his sufferings, the answer to his prayers, and surely worth the suffering and imprisonment he was enduring. It is the mystery of God's grace, working through Paul's acceptance of the way of the cross.

Paul used his imprisonment to testify to the good news of Jesus Christ. He transformed his suffering by allowing the message of the Gospel to be proclaimed in his life. In this way, he encouraged the persecuted communities, and attracted thousands of people to the Gospel. He used the title, "the prisoner of Christ Jesus," (in Philemon 1,9; Eph.

---

* The barracks for the bodyguard soldiers of the emperor.

3:11, 4:1; 2 Tim. 1:8) to remind the communities just where discipleship to Jesus Christ might lead.

Because Christians were imprisoned on a nearly daily basis, Paul—and subsequent writers who used his name—endeavored to encourage Christians to remain faithful and strong, to keep the faith in the hour of persecution which would surely come. Paul does not want his brothers and sisters to give up the struggle against the powers and the principalities, even if that means risking imprisonment and death. Stand firm, he insists. Let the witness of nonviolence carry on from your prison cell.

Nearly two thousand years later, Paul's message remains very hard for us to hear. Most of us today cannot imagine being imprisoned or killed for our faith. But for the early Christian community, Paul's words were authentic, rooted in necessity and encouraging.

The Example of Gandhi in prison

The person who has done the most in modern history to demonstrate the redemptive value of the nonviolent witness continued in prison is Mohandas Gandhi. Like Paul, Gandhi knew well that the pursuit of nonviolence—even to prison and the sacrifice of one's life—would blossom into a spirit of liberation, touching the hearts of many with a transforming grace. It is the same spirit which can, in the end, transform the world.

Gandhi felt this potential to be so great that, much like Paul, he invited the masses of Indians to risk prison as the road to their spiritual and actual liberation. His logic was the logic of nonviolent, sacramental civil disobedience:

> Civil disobedience is the storehouse of power. Imagine a whole people unwilling to conform to the laws of the legislature, and prepared to suffer the consequences of non-compliance! They will bring the whole legislative and executive machinery to a standstill. The police and the military are of use to coerce minorities, however powerful they may be. But no police or military coercion can bend the resolute will of a people who are out for suffering to the uttermost.[12]

In that spirit, Gandhi always sent a congratulatory telegram to his friends and colleagues as soon as he heard that they had gone to jail for their nonviolent civil disobedience. His attitude was indeed revolutionary:

> We must widen the prison gates and we must enter them as a bridegroom enters the bride's chamber. Freedom is to be wooed only inside prison walls and sometimes on gallows, never in the council chambers, courts, or the schoolroom.[13]

For Gandhi, "the cell door is the door to freedom." Going to prison was an essential component of Gandhi's nonviolent struggle for justice and peace. For Gandhi, true peacemaking required the sacrifice of one's freedom and life. Gandhi first went to jail on January 11, 1908, for a two-month sentence after refusing to 'register' as an Indian according to South Africa's racist laws.

He wrote at the time that "the prison authorities were friendly, the meals bad, and the cells over crowded." In the mornings, he read from the Bhagavad Gita and at noon from the Koran. He taught English from the Bible to a Chinese prisoner, and spent much time reading from Tolstoy, Socrates and Ruskin, among others. "Whoever has a taste for reading good books is able to bear loneliness in any place with great ease," he commented.

One day, while still in prison uniform, Gandhi was brought from his cell to the office of the South African president to negotiate the repeal of the registration laws. Gandhi's just cause and steadfast nonviolence compelled the head of the government to meet with him. An agreement was reached and Gandhi was immediately freed by the president himself. The hundreds of other nonviolent resisters were released the next day. That event sealed Gandhi's conviction that a steadfast, nonviolent stance for justice—continued in prison—would ultimately bear good fruit.

On October 10, 1908, Gandhi was again sentenced to two months in jail, and assigned to cook, clean toilets and dig ditches. When asked in a movement newsletter why he did not simply pay the fine and go home, Gandhi wrote from prison that "such thoughts make one really a coward."

Jail has its good sides, he argued. Peaceful contemplation and the continuing experiment in nonviolence can be spiritually beneficial, he firmly believed. In prison, there is only one warden, whereas in the free life there are many. One does not have to worry about food and the work keeps the body healthy. "The prisoner's soul is thus free and he has time to pray to God." Indeed, he concluded, "the real road to happiness lies in going to jail and undergoing sufferings and privations there in the interest of one's country and religion."[14]

When Gandhi began a long sentence in Yeravda Prison in 1924, after years of hectic organizing and public speaking, he wrote that he was grateful "finally to get some rest and still feel that I was serving the country, if possibly, more than when I was traveling up and down addressing huge audiences":

> I wish I could convince the workers that imprisonment of a comrade does not mean so much loss of work for a common cause. If we believe, as we have so often proclaimed we do, that unprovoked suffering is the surest way of remedying a wrong in regard to which the suffering is gone through, surely it follows as a matter of course that imprisonment of a comrade is no loss.
>
> Silent suffering, undergone with dignity and humility, speaks with an unrivaled eloquence. It is solid work because there is no ostentation about it. It is always true because there is no danger of miscalculation. Moreover, if we are true workers, the loss of a fellow-worker increases our zest and, therefore, capacity for work. And so long as we regard anybody as irreplaceable, we have not fitted ourselves for organized work. For organized

work means capacity for carrying it on in spite of depletion in the ranks. Therefore, we must rejoice in the unmerited suffering of friends or ourselves and trust that the cause, if it is just, will prosper through such suffering.[15]

After the 1932 Salt March, when Gandhi lead thousands to the Indian ocean to "make salt" in revolutionary opposition to British salt laws, Gandhi was sent back to the Yeravda prison, which he now referred to as "the Yeravda Temple." "I have been quite happy and making up for arrears in sleep," he wrote a week after he arrived.

In an effort to make Gandhi feel more comfortable, the jail superintendent ordered special furniture and cooking equipment to be set up in Gandhi's room, but Gandhi asked that it be removed.

Just as he had tutored the prison guards in various indigenous languages while imprisoned during the 1920s, Gandhi once again started tutoring the guards. After years together, several of the guards became very good friends with Gandhi.

Gandhi's wife of sixty-two years, Kasturbai, died while he was imprisoned; so did his personal secretary and friend, Mahadev Desai. Gandhi himself almost died there on several occasions. He knew prison life inside out, and continued to court it for the rest of his life.

Altogether, Gandhi spent 2,089 days in Indian prisons and 249 days in South African jails, a total of 2,338 days or nearly six-and-a-half years behind bars. After Gandhi's death, a professor from Oxford wrote that Gandhi's life sent a message to governments around the world:

> Be careful in dealing with a person who cares nothing for sensual pleasures, nothing for comfort or praise or promotion, but is simply determined to do what he or she believes to be right. He is a dangerous and uncomfortable enemy because his body, which you can always conquer, gives you so little purchase over his soul.[16]

Gandhi's civil disobedience and joyful willingness to risk prison, even death, stemmed from a revolutionary spirit that insisted on withdrawing cooperation from an unjust system of government. His steadfast belief in truth and nonviolence—in God, and God's spiritual way of redemptive suffering—convinced him that the illegal movement of civil disobedience would bear fruit, come what may.

"Civil disobedience becomes a sacred duty when the state has become lawless or corrupt, which is the same thing," Gandhi wrote. "As larger and larger numbers of innocent people come out to welcome death [or prison], their sacrifice will become the potent instrument for the salvation of all others, and there will be a minimum of suffering. Suffering cheerfully endured ceases to be suffering and is transmuted into an ineffable joy."[17]

"Imprisonments are courted because we consider it to be wrong to be free under a government we hold to be wholly bad," Gandhi insisted. "A government that is evil has no room for good men and women except in prisons."

Given the necessity to oppose injustice, Gandhi's prime motive nevertheless remained spiritual:

Self-purification is the main consideration in seeking prison. Embarrassment of the government is a secondary consideration. It is my unalterable conviction that even though the government may not feel embarrassed in any way whatsoever by the incarceration or even execution of an innocent unknown but purified person, such incarceration will be the end of the government. Even a single lamp dispels the deepest darkness.[18]

"For me," he added, "solitary confinement in a prison cell—without any breach on my part of the code of non-cooperation or private or public morals—will be freedom.

With this conviction, Gandhi continued to study his religious tradition while in prison. Hindu teachings on nonviolence and self-renunciation guided Gandhi throughout his years there. Gandhi's constant effort to plumb the depths of the Hindu tradition while he was in prison, enabled his prison witness to become sacramental, sacred.

He subsequently wrote essays like *How to Enjoy Jail*, and advised nonviolent resisters to "train themselves to feel happy" so they would always be happy in the lifelong struggle. "Just as everyone trains himself to do without things when he cannot get them, a follower of the Gita *dharam* [duty] trains himself to do without things with happiness... for the happiness of the Gita is not the opposite of unhappiness. It is superior to that state. The devotee of the Gita is neither happy nor unhappy. And when that state is reached, there is no pain, no pleasure, no victory, no defeat, no deprivation, no possession. Prison life is a life of privilege if we learn to practice the Gita teachings." He continued:

> We must make the best possible use of the invaluable leisure in jail. Perhaps the best of uses would be to cultivate the power of independent thought. We are often thoughtless and therefore like only to read books or worse still, to talk.
>
> As a matter of fact, there is an art of thinking just as there is an art of reading. We should be able to think the right thought at the right time and not indulge in thinking useless thoughts as well as in reading useless books. It is my experience during every incarceration that it affords us a fine opportunity of thinking to some purpose.[19]

Gandhi's way of nonviolence also included a disciplined cooperation with jail authorities, so long as they did not force resisters to act unjustly or use violence. In 1924, he wrote that, based on his own prison experience, all imprisoned resisters are bound by the basic principles of *satyagraha* (or "truth-force"):

1. To act with the most scrupulous honesty;
2. To cooperate with the prison officials in their administration;

3. To set by our obedience to all reasonable discipline an example to co-prisoners;

4. To ask for no favors and claim no privileges which the meanest prisoners do not get and which we do not need strictly for reasons of health;

5. Not to fail to ask what we do so need and not to get irritated if we do not obtain it;

6. To do all the tasks allotted, to the utmost of our ability.

It is such conduct which will make the government position uncomfortable and untenable...They have not yet found out any way of dealing with nonviolence save by yielding to it. The idea behind the imprisonment of *satyagrahis* is that he expects relief through humble submission to suffering. He believes that meek suffering for a just cause has a virtue all its own and infinitely greater than the virtue of the sword.

This does not mean that we may not resist when the treatment touches our self-respect. Thus for instance, we must resist to the point of death the use of abusive language by officials or if they were to throw our food at us, which is often done. Insult and abuse are no part of an official's duty. Therefore we must resist them.[20]

"Jail discipline must be submitted to until jail government itself becomes or is felt to be corrupt or immoral," Gandhi wrote from prison. He continued:

But deprivation of comfort, imposition of restrictions and such other inconveniences do not make jail government corrupt. It becomes that when prisoners are humiliated or treated with inhumanity as when they are kept in filthy dens or are given food unfit for human consumption. Indeed, I hope that the conduct of non-cooperators in the jail will be strictly correct, dignified and yet submissive.

We must not regard jailers and wardens as our enemies, but as fellow human beings not utterly devoid of the human touch. Our gentle behavior is bound to disarm all suspicion or bitterness. I know that this path of discipline on the one hand and fierce defiance on the other is a very difficult path, but there is no royal road to [freedom]. The country has deliberately chosen the narrow road and the straight path. Like a straight line, it is the shortest distance. But even as you require a steady and experienced hand to draw a straight line, so are steadiness of discipline and firmness of purpose absolutely necessary if we are to walk along the chosen path with an unerring step.[21]

Inside the jail, by his exemplary conduct, [the nonviolent resister] reforms even the criminals surrounding him [or her]; he [or she] softens the hearts of jailers and others in authority. Such meek behavior springing from strength and knowledge ultimately dissolves the tyranny of the tyrant. It is for this reason that I claim that voluntary suffering is the quickest and the best remedy for the removal of abuses and injustices.[22]

The long night of Thoreau: Gandhi's inspiration

One of Gandhi's most inspiring heroes was Henry David Thoreau, the author of *Walden*, who refused to pay taxes and was subsequently jailed for one night. Thoreau's experience bore tremendous fruit in the peace of his own soul, and subsequently, in his famous essay, *On the Duty of Civil Disobedience*:

l was put into a jail once [for not paying taxes], for one night; and, as l stood considering the walls of solid stone, two or three feet thick, the door of wood and iron, a foot thick, and the iron grating which strained the light, I could not help being struck with the foolishness of that institution which treated me as if l were mere flesh and blood and bones, to be locked up.

l wondered that it should have concluded at length that this was the best use it could put me to, and had never thought to avail itself of my services in some way. l saw that, if there was a wall of stone between me and my townsmen, there was a still more difficult one to climb or break through, before they could get to be as free as l was. l did not feel for a moment confined, and the walls seemed a great waste of stone and mortar. l felt as if l alone of all my townsmen paid my tax. They plainly did not know how to treat me... In every threat and in every compliment there was a blunder; for they thought that my chief desire was to stand the other side of that wall. As they could not reach me, they had resolved to punish my body.[23]

Thoreau's lone example, and articulate reflection published afterwards, paved the way for generations of resisters to come. His sacramental insight into interior freedom—felt while imprisoned for his conscience—speaks to us today of the possibilities of the human soul to spark the transformation of the world. His witness is still bearing fruit.

The solitary witness of Franz Jaegerstaetter

Franz Jaegerstaetter was an Austrian peasant who was beheaded on August 9, 1943, by the Nazis for refusing to fight for them. His long, lonely, nonviolent resistance led to several years imprisonment before his execution. For Jaegerstaetter, resistance was a matter of faith. It was a spiritual issue. Thus, his days in a Nazi prison were days of prayer and contemplation. He wrote to his wife from prison, shortly before his death:

> You should not be sad because of my present situation. For we cannot know God's mind or which of the many paths [God] leaves us to travel and still reach the right goal. As long as a person has an untroubled conscience and knows that he is not really a criminal, he can live at peace even in prison.[24]

The priest who visited him the night before he was executed said later that Franz's eyes shone with a deep calm, peace and joy. On a table in Franz's cell lay a document which he had only to sign to save his life. When the priest suggested he sign it, Franz Jaegerstaetter "smiled" and "pushed it aside," saying, "I cannot and may not take an oath in favor of a government that is fighting an unjust war."

He received the sacraments of the Catholic Church, and when offered some spiritual reading materials, declined saying, "I am completely bound in union with God, and any reading would only interrupt my communication with God." Later, the priest told a group of Sisters, "I can only congratulate you on this countryman of yours who lived as a saint and has now died a hero. I say with certainty that this simple man is the only saint that I have ever met in my lifetime."

Jaegerstaetter's spiritual witness and steadfast nonviolence give one of the brightest examples of sacramental civil disobedience in the twentieth century. His example harkens back to the testimonies and martyrdoms of the early Christians. He serves as a model for all who are imprisoned for their faith, their conscience, and their hunger for peace and justice.

The prophetic voice of Martin Luther King Jr. in jail

Dr. King spent several weeks during his short lifetime in jail as the consequence of his nineteen arrests. King always encouraged congregations and audiences to take the risk of nonviolent civil disobedience, as a means of joining the movement for civil rights and peace.

"Nobody wants to go to jail," he preached, "but if they put you in jail, transform it from a dungeon of despair into an oasis of peace and justice."[25] In his historic essay, *Letter from a Birmingham Jail*, written in April, 1963, King described his effort to spread the gospel of racial equality and justice. He described his willingness to suffer in the spirit of redemptive love so that people could be converted and transformed into brothers and sisters, living in peace. He wrote:

> I am in Birmingham because injustice is here. Just as
> the eighth century prophets left their little villages
> and carried their "thus saith the Lord" far beyond the
> boundaries of their hometowns; and just as the Apostle
> Paul left his little village of Tarsus and carried the gospel
> of Jesus Christ to practically every hamlet and city of
> the Greco-Roman world, I too am compelled to carry
> the gospel of freedom beyond my particular hometown.
> Like Paul, I must constantly respond to the Macedonian
> call for aid.[26]

Like Paul, Dr. King suffered every form of accusation and persecution. King knew well the folly of the cross—that millions of people would see his suffering, accepted in Christ's love for justice and peace, and that they would then take up the Gospel struggle for social change, in the same spirit as the unarmed, risen Christ.

William Robert Miller, director of the Fellowship of Reconciliation from 1956-1962, summed up this insight concerning the redemptive value of resistance in his book, *Nonviolence*:

> More people can be swayed by the simple fact of suffering than by a righteous cause that does not vitally affect them. Our going to jail may bring the issue to life for them and cause them to exert pressure on those who make policy. Officials who imagined that they were only maintaining law and order may see themselves cast in the role of oppressors and find the image uncomfortable, leading them to rethink their position.
>
> Even among the opponent's masses there may be a change of attitude. Going to jail potentially raises the question whether the offense at issue is so vital to the existence of the opponent's way of life that its whole system of law enforcement must be made to hinge on it.[27]

Perhaps even more than Gandhi, King showed the whole world the spiritual and practical potential of sacramental civil disobedience and the nonviolent witness in prison. Through his own suffering, imprisonments and eventual martyrdom, King motivated and challenged millions to take a stand for justice and peace. His legacy invites us to carry on where he left off.

The lifelong commitment of Dorothy Day

Dorothy Day was the co-founder of the Catholic Worker movement, the editor of the *Catholic Worker* newspaper.

But her first act of nonviolent civil disobedience occurred in 1917, almost fifteen years before she began the Worker movement with Peter Maurin: Day was arrested outside the White House for picketing with other suffragists, and spent thirty days in Virginia's Occoquan penitentiary. Several of the suffragists were kept in solitary confinement.

In the late 1950s, she served four jail sentences, including another thirty days, for refusing to take shelter during a New York City nuclear war air raid drill. Her public civil disobedience helped to bring an end to those drills.

"I have been behind bars in police stations, houses of detention, jails and prison farms eleven times, and have refused to pay federal income taxes and have never voted," she remembered towards the end of her life. "The whole experience of jail was good for my soul." After twenty-five days in the New York Women's House of Detention in October, 1957, she wrote:

> One comes out from jail into a world where everyone has problems, all but insoluble problems, and the first thing that strikes me is that the world today is almost worse than jail. Looking at newspapers, listening to the radio, even watching the activities of children, and thinking fearfully of what they have to look forward to in the way of education, work, and war, I am appalled...
>
> [This] is what we did when we went to jail. We were setting our faces against the world, against things as they are, the terrible injustice of our capitalist industrial system which lives by war and by preparing for war;

setting our faces against race hatreds and all nationalist
strivings. But especially we wanted to act against
war and the preparation for war: nerve gas, guided
missiles, the testing and stockpiling of nuclear bombs,
conscription, the collection of income tax—against
the entire military state. We made our gesture; we
disobeyed a law.[28]

"Going to jail is dying to oneself and living according to
the great commandment of Jesus," Dorothy Day believed,
"not only loving your neighbor as yourself, but loving them
enough to lay down your life for them." She summed up her
philosophy with a simple declaration of faith:

When I lay in jail thinking of these things, thinking
of war and peace and the problem of human freedom,
of jails, drug addiction, prostitution, and the apathy
of great masses of people who believe that nothing
can be done—when I thought of these things, I was all
the more confirmed in my faith in the little way of St.
Therese. We do the minute things that come to hand,
we pray our prayers, and beg also for an increase of
faith—and God will do the rest.[29]

During the war, when she was asked, what could be done,
Day responded, "We should fill the jails with young men
refusing to go off and fight."[30]

Dorothy Day knew the power of sacramental nonviolence.
For her, it was simply the power of God at work in us to
change the world. She trusted that God's Spirit would

transform us all so that the reign of God would one day be realized on earth. Her very life became a sacramental revelation of that reign.

The steadfast stand of Philip Berrigan

Philip Berrigan and three friends shocked the nation in 1967 by pouring their blood over draft records in a Baltimore recruiting office. After he was out on parole, he organized the Catonsville Nine draft board action.

By 1994, he had spent over seven years of his life behind bars for his stand against war. His years in prison, he believed, were a small price to pay for the transformation that still must occur in our country. Berrigan maintained that transformation will only come about through the nonviolent presence of resisters, keeping vigil in jail—as he once wrote from prison:

> If I were the lowliest of draft resisters, buried anonymously in some federal prison, forgotten by everyone but parents and one or two friends, I would be contributing more to the building of peace than the most spectacular dove, who makes headlines and rallies supporters, and whose exhortations are heard with apprehension even in the halls of government.
>
> "Yet to shame the wise, God has chosen what the world counts folly, and to shame what is strong, God has chosen what the world counts weakness. He has chosen things low and contemptible, mere nothings, to

overthrow the existing order. And so there is no place for human pride in the presence of God."(I Cor. 1:27-29).[31]

When asked by a visiting prison psychiatrist why he risked imprisonment—why he did not simply leave the country or go underground—Berrigan responded: "Because we will survive only if people pay the price of survival. At this stage I may help them more to change through an extravagant sentence than by doing what you suggest. Furthermore, we need to learn much about the role of prison in nonviolent revolution."

When a nonviolent resister has become "indifferent to jail, separation, loneliness, humiliation, loss of financial security and career satisfaction," then he or she has become a true peacemaker, Berrigan wrote.[32]

While in the Robeson County Jail in North Carolina for the 'Pax Christi—Spirit of Life Plowshares action' of which I was a part, Berrgian wrote that "jail for us is a way of subverting society":

Jail is a way of disarming a society that builds nuclear weapons and indulges in perpetual war-making. Jail unites us with the poor, confronting a society that manufactures destitution and homelessness. Jail is subversive of a society that in one way or another manages to shackle the conscience of even its favorites. Mark declares at the beginning of his gospel that social change comes from "the wilderness." John the Baptizer emerges from that unlikely setting, as did Jesus.

Today the "wilderness" includes...the jails and prisons across the land. There, resisters appeal to the hearts and minds of others, whether in or out, and testify against the criminality of public authority. The Robeson County Jail is one of the worst ever. We are lodged in a dustbin where it is all but impossible to obtain a book or a change of clothing. Lynn Fredriksson (our co-defendant) did three weeks in solitary, unable to bear the heavy smoking of the women's cell block. She is now in a smoke-free block. We three men are blessed in being together for Bible reflection and good talk, when the TV is not at top volume.

No one of us likes jail. No one in their right mind would seek it. But God's word and the strenuous work of community are sufficient for us. We transcend this pit of misery; we shrug, grin and bear it. In measure, we help humanize it. Meantime, in the so-called real world, the Clinton administration sounds the war tocsin against North Korea. A perennial worldwide search is on for that all but vanished species, 'the enemy'.

As for slavish concessions to the Pentagon, President Clinton outpaces former President Bush by a mile—in arms sales, fiscal support, new weapons systems and a belligerent ideology to match. The rich are reassured. The weapons are in place. In this morally polluted atmosphere, we believe that imprisonment could hardly be more to the point. We shudder under the blows of a society permanently mobilized against peace. Duplicity, propaganda, media indifference, and institutional betrayal mark our plight.

Let us not give up. Let us continue to nourish one another by consistent and prayerful presence at military installations, in courts and lockups. Indeed, we need to be free enough to go to jail. We need to fill up the jails. Nonviolent revolution will come out of the wilderness, as it always has.[33]

Phil Berrigan continued his steadfast witness for peace over decades of nonviolent civil disobedience, including several Plowshares actions. Like Dorothy Day, he called upon all Christians to "fill the jails" in order to stop the US war machine.

The peacemaking soul of Daniel Berrigan

"Prison is paradoxically a place where the peace Jesus promises can take root in one's life and grow," wrote Daniel Berrigan from Danbury Federal Prison, where he spent two years, beginning in August, 1970, for his participation in the Catonsville Nine draft-board raid against the US war in Vietnam.

His prison diary, *Lights On In the House of the Dead*, records his day to day experience of despair and hope. "If jail is the great seizure of humanity by the death force of the state, then every assertion of life, goodness, cheerfulness, friendship is glue in the locks no key may enter and claim".

Berrigan wrote on October 7, 1970: "If the state is a death mechanism, it is up to us to live here, and to give life, and to measure the passage of days, as well as our failure and growth, by the life we lead. If 'freemen' make war, it is up to caged men and women to disclaim war, in their immediate dealings; and thus deal another hand."

On October 20, 1970, he listed his hopes and prayers, the insights gained from prison life:

[I have learned] That what we do, what we endure, will have meaning for others. That our lives are not wasted, in the measure in which we give them. That the giving of our lives is a concrete, simple task; at center eye, the men we live with and suffer among and strive to serve. That life in jail, in proportion to one's awareness, has powerful analogies with 'life outside' to the inquiring mind and the contemplative heart.

That to be fools for Christ's sake is a responsible political position, given the rampant death society, its irresponsibility and horror of life. That we are called, as prisoners, to be disciplined, prayerful, constant, vigilant over sense and appetite, cheerful and of good heart.

That relief of inequity, inhumanity, and injustice are present and pressing tasks. The struggle goes on here too. That powerlessness is a way which offers solidarity and concurrent action with all those who struggle and endure in the world. That in prison we are in communion not only with suffering men and women of our world, but with the communion of saints in every time and place. That our jailers also lie under the scrutiny as well as the saving will of God, and stand in great need of our compassion and our courtesy...

That we are called to live the mystery of the cross
and to sweat through the mystery of the resurrection.
That we accept first, in body and spirit, our conviction
that human conditions must worsen, that there is more
to be endured than we have so far endured, before
amelioration comes. That good humor and riding easy
are the saving salt of our condition. We may win big,
we may win small, we may lose everything. We can take
whichever outcome. Important: stand where you must
stand, be human there.[34]

"In a true sense," Berrigan wrote a few weeks later, "it can
be said of Philip and me that we have nothing to do but
stand firm in these months—to survive, to act as a silent
prick to the consciousness of those outside whether of
friend or opponent, church or state."

"How to believe that our being here is making a difference
for others?" he asked himself on March 16, 1971. "We are to
believe, as I do most firmly, that being here is the natural
crown of everything that went before; not merely in a
humanistic sense that good people inevitably come to ill,
but in the sense of the crowning of a journey of faith by the
opening of a wider vista of faith. The reward of faith, that
is to say, is not vision, it is a life which both requires and
bestows a greater measure of faith; the ability to see the
journey through, stage by stage, so that the promise, still
withheld, remains itself, pristine, never cancelled."

"I feel at peace, a strange feeling, one to be grateful for
while it lasts," he wrote on August 6, 1971. "The penance of

life here is incomparable in the bonds it offers us with the other prisoners."

In characteristic good humor, Daniel Berrigan began his diary by explaining his experience of prison as "an eighteen-month Live-in Grant conferred on the author by the US government":

The author was invited to begin serving his residency in April of 1970. Ordinarily in accepting the grant, applicants are required to take up residence at Danbury on the agreed date. However, in this case, the April assignment was judged inconvenient and the author invoked *epikeia* from the common law, due to unfinished business. A vivid disagreement ensued, that wrestling which is the very soul of art. Finally, having consummated various unfinished businesses here and there, the author took up residence in the Connecticut hills in August of 1970.[35]

Though his days in prison were extremely difficult (he nearly died at one point), Daniel Berrigan emerged to speak out anew against war and for peace. Like his brother Phil, he remained faithful to the Gospel, continuing to celebrate the sacrament of civil disobedience until his death.

Epilogue

Keeping the faith: a Plowshares story

When Phil Berrigan, Lynn Fredriksson, Bruce Friedrich and I walked through the middle of wargames at the Seymour Johnson Air Force Base in Goldsboro, North Carolina on December 7th, 1993, and hammered on an FI SE nuclear fighter bomber, we were trying to symbolically and literally begin anew the process of disarmament. But during the trials and the eight months in jail that followed, I began to realize more and more how this act of nonviolent civil disobedience was for me an act of faith.

As we stepped onto the base, I felt challenged to get beyond my paralyzing fear, and walk in faith. As I hammered on the nuclear bomber in our 'Pax Christi— Spirit of Life Plowshares' action, I sensed that the God of peace was indeed with us. As I endured jail, I believed that my confinement and suffering would bear fruit.

Many people have asked me why I participated in this dramatic act of civil disobedience. Though the Cold War is over, the Berlin wall is down, communism has collapsed and the Soviet Union has disintegrated, still I answer, as long as we possess one nuclear weapon, we are in danger. In reality, we possess thousands of them. We are still wedded to violence as the only solution to the world's problems.

Instead of pursuing peace and justice for the poor, we prefer to spend billions annually on weapons of war while the poor of the world starve and die in poverty. Not only were we trying to stop the killing which is warfare, but we were pointing out how the massive US military arsenal is connected to the poverty and oppression of the developing world.

The money spent on these weapons belongs to the poor of the world. In order to have justice for the poor, we need to dismantle our weapons, renounce war, and start spending our resources on food, healthcare, education, homes, and jobs for all the world's poor. Our action pinponted the heart of our world's problems and proposed an answer. *Disarmament*, we declared, is the solution to the world's ills.

Today, the larger, critical issue of the climate crisis may make this seem more complex, more urgent; yet the spirit is the same. 'Inaction' by governments is harder to identify and makes protest more complicated, perhaps, than the protest against weapons of war; but it is violence, against the earth and against the poor, which is in question.*

"Governments never disarm; only people do," Phil said to us one morning in jail, while we were reflecting on our action. "Governments disarm only because their people insist on disarmament." Likewise, disarmament and justice will only come if people are willing to sacrifice for it. We

---

* Furthermore, making and renewing weapons entails the emission of vast amounts of pollutants—and these are usually not counted in a country's carbon budget, nor indeed are any of the emissions produced by the military in its different areas of activity. It is all interconnected.

insist that our nation disarm, and we are willing to suffer the consequences for our public, nonviolent insistence.

How effective was your action? reporters ask us. I reply that we are just trying to take seriously God's commandment to disarm, to stop the killing and to love one another. We are seeking to be faithful to the God of peace. For me, our action was more than a political act; it was an experiment in the truth of Gospel nonviolence. I was trying to take seriously the commands of God in the scriptures: "Thou shalt not kill" (Dt. 5:17); "Beat Swords into Plowshares" (Is. 2:4); and "Love your enemies" (Mt.5:44). I was trying to heed Jesus' words and take up the cross of nonviolent resistance.

Was your action successful? they ask. We leave the results and the outcome in God's hands. Our unarmed God teaches us that these weapons of mass destruction should not exist; that they are a perversion of God's creation; that they are anti-God, anti-life, and anti-property; that they rob the poor; and that they prepare and make possible the nuclear crucifixion of humanity.

We have done what we could. We have taken a prayerful stand for peace. Like any sacrament, our action cannot be measured in results or effectiveness. It can only be experienced as transforming grace, as the presence of God moving among us. We trust that it will bear fruit, that one day, thousands of people will come forward and dismantle every nuclear weapon on the earth, that one day, war will be abolished and people will commit themselves to nonviolence, justice and peace.

As we sat in the confines of our county jail cell, I felt the guiding hand of God. Each morning in jail, Phil, Bruce and I spent two to three hours studying the Gospel of Mark. Afterwards, we celebrated a simple Eucharist with Wonder bread and grape juice. We offered the Lord's prayer and exchanged a sign of peace. We felt the presence of the risen Jesus in our midst. We shared a living solidarity with the poor and oppressed (particularly Black Americans).

Though we were never brought outdoors in all those many months in jail, we were sustained by the grace of the scriptures, community, and prayer. Jail became for me a place to "keep watch," as the Gospel of Mark suggests (Mk.14:34).

Our Plowshares action, arrest, trial and imprisonment were very difficult experiences for me, but they were also a great blessing. My whole life was turned upside-down. All at once, from my jail cell, I was plunged back to the basics of Christianity: faith, hope, love, compassion, contemplation, truth, powerlessness, suffering, resistance, voluntary poverty, community, persecution, humiliation, humility and trust. As we resist war and death, I am learning, we discover anew the meaning of peace and life.

The only way to peace, justice and disarmament is through the voluntary acceptance of suffering. The only way to promote positive social change, for a person of faith, is to pass through the paschal mystery, just as Jesus did. Our action and our imprisonment were not just experiences of the cross; they were also sharings in the resurrection.

As Phil, Bruce and I endured months in a small jail cell, we felt like Shadrach, Meshach, and Abednego, cast into the fiery furnace for refusing to worship the empire's idols (Daniel 3:1-28). Despite the flames around us, we were unharmed. Indeed, we were blessed with the presence of God in our midst. As an experience of faith, our civil disobedience was sacramental.

Like the vigilant Jesus praying in the Garden of Gethsemane and waiting for the soldiers to arrive, we are all called to speak the truth, act nonviolently, resist the structures of oppression and prayerfully await the outcome, even if that means arrest, trial, imprisonment and death— as well as the other outcome, the coming of God's reign of nonviolent love and justice.

We will resist with Christ and wait with Christ for the consequences of our active nonviolence. We are learning to follow Christ to the cross and to the resurrection. As we engage in sacramental civil disobedience, in obedience to God's law of nonviolent love, we will find peace. We will experience the loving presence of the God of peace and for a moment, we will be transformed. As this subversive grace transformed even us, so will it transform the world.

References

Introduction

1   Martos, Joseph, *Doors to the Sacred* (New York: Image Books, 1982), p. 7.

2   Dear, John, *They Will Inherit the Earth* (New York: Orbis Books, 2018), pp.45-46.

A Different Way is Possible

1   Thoreau, Henry David, "On the Duty of Civil Disobedience" in *Walden and Civil Disobedience* (New York: New American Library, 1960), p. 230.

2   Montgomery, Anne, "Divine Obedience," in Laffin, Arthur J. and Montgomery, Anne, *Swords into Plowshares* (San Francisco: Harper and Row, 1987), p. 25.

3   King, Martin Luther, "Letter from a Birmingham Jail," in Washington, James (Ed.), *A Testament of Hope: The Essential Writings of Martin Luther King, Jr.* (San Francisco: Harper and Row, 1986), pp. 293-294.

4   Berrigan, Philip, "On Blindness and Healing," in *Swords into Plowshares*, ibid., pp. 51- 53.

5   McAlister, Elizabeth, "A Community of Sanity," in *Sojourners* May, 1983, pp. 28-29. (Emphasis added)

6   Merton,Thomas, *The Nonviolent Alternative*, (New York: Farrar Straus, Giroux, 1971), p. 233.

7   Zahn, Gordan, "Original Child Monk," in *The Nonviolent Alternative*, ibid., p. xxxvii.

8   King, *op. cit.*, pp. 240-242.

9   Douglass, James, "A Leaven in the Leaven," in *Sojourners*, May, 1983, pp. 23-24; and "Loving Disobedience," in *Ground Zero*, May-June 1982, p. 6.

We Will Not Serve Your False God

1   Myers, Ched, "By What Authority: The Bible and Civil Disobedience," *Sojourners*, May, 1984, p. 11.

2   Cicchino, Peter, "Toward a Theology of Advocacy" June, 1989, (Unpublished), pp. 21-23; and Walsh, James, *The Mighty from Their Thrones* (Phil: Fortress Press, 1987).

3   Myers, *op. cit.*, p. 11.

4   Daube, David, *Civil Disobedience in Antiquity* (Edinburgh: Edinburgh University Press, 1972), p. 5; also, Myers, *op. cit.*, p. 11.

5   Myers, *op. cit.*, p. 11.

6   Daube, *op. cit.*, p. 5.

7   Myers, *op. cit.*, p. 12.

8   Daube *op. cit.*, pp. 70-71.

9   Myers, *op. cit.*, p. 12

10 Daube, *op. cit.*, p. 82.

11 Berrigan, Daniel, "Unflinching Faith," in *The Other Side*, September-October, 1990, p. 10.

12 Washington, James (Ed.), *A Testament of Hope: The Essential Writings of Martin Luther King, Jr.* (San Francisco: Harper and Row, 1986), p. 294.

13 Daube, *op. cit.*, p. 84.

14 Myers, *op. cit.*, p.12.; and Collins, J., *The Apocalyptic Vision of the Book of Daniel* (Missoula: Scholars Press, 1977), p. 213.

15 Myers, Ched, *Binding the Strong Man* (Maryknoll, NY: Orbis Books, 1988), p. 391.

The Revolution of Nonviolence is at Hand

1 Merton, Thomas, *Gandhi on Nonviolence* (New York: New Directions, 1964), p. 40.

2 Ahn Byung Mu, "Jesus and the Minjung in the Gospel of Mark," in Kim Yong Bok (Ed.), *Minjung Theology* (Singapore: The Commission on Theological Concerns, 1981), pp. 142-143.

3 Myers, Ched, *Binding the Strong Man* (Maryknoll: Orbis Books, 1988), p. 161.

4 Kellermann, Bill, "The Cleansing of the Temple," in Wallis, Jim (Ed.), *The Rise of Christian Conscience* (San Francisco: Harper and Row, 1987), p. 258.

5 *Ibid.*, pp. 258-259.

6 Myers, *op. cit.*, p. 80.

7 Kellermann, *op. cit.*, p. 259.

8 Myers, *op. cit.*, pp. 299-302.

We Must Obey God Rather Than People

1 For an excellent commentary on The Acts of the Apostles, see Berrigan, Daniel, *Whereon to Stand: The Acts of the Apostles and Ourselves* (Fortkamp Pub. Co., Baltimore, MD, 1993).

2 Stevick, Daniel, *Civil Disobedience and the Christian* (New York: Seabury Press, 1969), p. 31.

3 Myers, *op. cit.*, p. 244.

4 Stevick, *op. cit.*, p. 46 and p. 36.

5 Myers, *op. cit.*, p. 245.

6 *Ibid.*, p. 244.

7 Stevick, *op. cit.*, pp. 31-32.

8   Musto, Ronald, *The Catholic Peace Tradition* (Maryknoll: Orbis Books, 1986), p. 34.

9   *Ibid.*, p. 38.

10 Codaro, Tom, *To Wake the Nation* (Pax Christi USA, 348 East Tenth St., Erie, PA, 16503; Benet Press, 1989), p. 8.

11 Stevick, *op. cit.*, p. 45.

12 Musto, *op. cit.*, p. 39.

13 Stevick, *op. cit.*, p. 46.

14 McSorley, Richard, *New Testament Basis for Peacemaking* (Scottdale, PA: Herald Press 1985), p. 70.

15 Fahey, Joseph, *Peace, War, and the Christian Conscience* (New York: Christopher Publications, 1982), p. 2.

16 Musto, *op. cit.*, p. 39.

17 Stevick, *op. cit.*, p. 47.

18 McSorley, *op. cit.*, pp. 70-71.

19 Musto, *op. cit.*, p. 39.

20 McSorley, *op. cit.*, p. 73.

21 Musto, *op. cit.*, p. 44.

22 Taylor, Richard and Sider, Ronald, "Fighting Fire with Water: A Call for Assertive Nonviolent Resistance," in Wallis, Jim (Ed.), *The Rise of Christian Conscience* (San Francisco: Harper and Row, 1987), p. 201; see also, Cadoux, C.J., *The Early Church and the World* (Edinburgh: Clark, 1925).

23 McSorley, *op. cit.*, p. 75.

24 Musto, *op. cit.*, p. 44-45.

Blessing the Empire

1   Cadoux, C.J., *The Early Church and the World* (Edinburgh: Clark, 1925), p. 528.

2   Bainton, Roland, *Christian Attitudes Toward War and Peace*, (Nashville: Abingdon Press, 1960), p. 53.

3   Gilligan, John, "Teaching Peace in a Christian Context," in Rouner, Leroy (Ed.), *Celebrating Peace* (Notre Dame, IN: University of Notre Dame Press, 1990), p. 17.

4   Douglass, James, *The Nonviolent Cross* (New York: Macmillan, 1968), p. 56.

5   Berrigan, Daniel, *The Mission* (San Francisco: Harper and Row, 1986), p. 56.

6   Donahue, John, *Lecture on Romans 12-13* (Unpublished; Jesuit School of Theology, Berkeley, California, April 20, 1990).

7   Myers, Ched, "By What Authority," in Wallis, Jim (Ed.), *The Rise of Christian Conscience* (San Francisco: Harper and Row, 1987), p. 244

8   McCarthy, Charles, *Christian Nonviolence: Option or Obligation?* (Unpublished, 1984), pp. 12, 54.

9   Myers, Ched, *op. cit.*

10 Flaherty, James. "An Exegesis of Romans 13:1-7," (Unpublished; The Jesuit School of Theology, Berkeley, California; 1990), p. 3; see also: Dunn, James, "Romans 9-16" in Hubbard, David, and Barker, Glenn (Eds.), *The Word Biblical Commentary* (Dallas: Word Books, 1988), Vol. 38B, pp. 765-766.

11 See Furnish, Victor, *The Moral Teaching of Paul: Selected Issues* (Nashville: Abingdon Press, 1985).

12 Stevick, *op. cit.*, pp. 25-29.

13 Douglass, James, *The Nonviolent Cross* (New York: Macmillan, 1968), pp. 207-208.

14 Merton, Thomas, *The Nonviolent Alternative* (New York: Farrar,

Straus, Girous, 1980), pp. 44-45.

15　Aquinas, Thomas, *Summa Theologiae* (II-II, Question 24, "Of Murder).

16　Douglass, *op. cit.*, p. 232.

17　*Ibid.*, p. 71.

A New History

1　Pope Francis, @Pontifex on Twitter, Sep 30, 2020, 12.55pm.

2　Berrigan, Daniel, "Merton, the Peacemaker" in Hart, Patrick (Ed.), *Thomas Merton: Monk* (Kalamazoo, Michigan: Cistercian Pub., 1983), p. 226.

3　Taylor, *op. cit.*, p. 250.

4　Taylor, Richard and Sider, Ronald, "Fighting Fire with Water," in Wallis, Jim (Ed.), *The Rise of Christian Conscience, op. cit.*, pp. 203-204.

5　Taylor, Richard and Sider, Ronald, *Nuclear Holocaust and Christian Hope* (Intervarsity Press), pp. 242-243.

6　Taylor, Richard and Sider, Ronald, "Fighting Fire with Water," *op. cit.*, p. 203.

7　Taylor, Richard, "With All Due Respect," *op. cit.*, p. 253.

8　Kemper, Vicki, "Peace Pentecost: It Won't Be Long Now," in Wallis, Jim (Ed.), *The Rise of Christian Conscience* (San Francisco: Harper and Row, 1987), p. 122.

There Comes a Time to Cross the Line

1　Douglass, James, "Civil Disobedience as Prayer" in Laffin, Arthur and Montgomery, Anne (Eds.), *Swords Into Plowshares* (San Francisco: Harper and Row, 1987), pp. 93-94.

2　*Ibid.,* p. 96.

3　Wallis, Jim, "A Higher Loyalty," *Sojourners*, May, 1983, pp. 5-6.

4 Douglass, *op. cit.*, pp. 96-97.

5 Stringfellow, William, *Free In Obedience* (New York: Seabury Press, 1964), p. 91.

6 Feuerherd, Peter. "Why Would Anybody Want to Get Arrested?" in *Salt*, September, 1988, p. 9.

7 Douglass, *op. cit.*, p. 97.

8 Du Plessix Gray, Francine, *Divine Disobedience: Profiles in Catholic Radicalism* (New York: Vintage Books, 1969), pp. 56-57.

9 Feuerherd, *op. cit.*, p. 9.

Preparing to Act

1 Meehan, Francis, *Pax Christi USA Statement on Civil Disobedience*, March, 1987. Available from Pax Christi USA, 348 East Tenth St., Erie, PA, 16503.

2 Kownacki, Mary Lou, "Letter to an Experimenter in Truth," *Sojourners*, May, 1983, p.28.

3 *Ibid.*

4 Meehan, *op. cit.*

5 Fleming, David (Ed.), *The Spiritual Exercises*, Institute of Jesuit Sources, St. Louis, 1978, p. 205.

6 Barry, William and Connolly, William, *The Practice of Spiritual Direction*, Harper and Row, San Francisco, 1982, p. 102.

7 Montgomery, Anne and Laffin, Arthur, *Swords into Plowshares* (San Francisco: Harper and Row, 1987), pp. 27-28.

8 *Ibid.*, pp. 30-31.

9 Written by John Dear and Jack Marth for a nonviolent witness against C.I.A. recruitment at Fordham University, Spring, 1986.

10 See Dear, John, *Disarming the Heart: Toward a Vow of Nonviolence* (Scottdale, PA: Herald Press, 1993).

11 Vanderhaar, Gerry, *Nonviolence: Theory and Practice* (Pax Christi USA, 1980), p. 8.

Anything Can Happen

1 Shannon, William, *Seeking the Face of God* (New York: Crossroad Pub., 1988), pp. 151- 156.

2 Oates, Stephen, *Let the Trumpet Sound*, (New York: New American Library, 1982), p. 220.

Testifying to the Truth

1 Fischer, Louis, *The Life of Mahatma Gandhi* (San Francisco: Harper and Row, 1950), p. 202.

2 Berrigan, Daniel, "Portrait of the Peacemaker as a Healer" in *The Other Side*, July/August, 1987, p. 14.

3 For a more complete essay on the trials and courtroom proceedings of the Plowshares movement and the lessons to be learned from their experiments in truth, see Mass, Elmer, "Disarmament on Trial," in Laffin, Arthur and Montgomery, Anne (Eds.), *Swords Into Plowshares* (San Francisco: Harper and Row, 1987), pp. 66-72.

4 Wallis, Jim (Ed.), *Peacemakers* (San Francisco: Harper and Row, 1983), pp. 148-150.

5 *Ibid.*, pp. 151-152.

6 Berrigan, Daniel, "Swords into Plowshares," in Laffin, Arthur and Montgomery, Anne (Eds.), *Swords into Plowshares, op. cit.*, p. 64.

7 Berrigan, Daniel, "Time Waiting, Time Served" in *Sojourners*, June, 1990, pp. 6-7.

8 Brockman, James, *Romero: A Life* (Maryknoll, NY: Orbis Books, 1989), pp. 241-242.

9 Boesak, Allan, "Your Days Are Over!" in Wallis, Jim (Ed.), *Crucible of Fire* (Maryknoll, NY: Orbis Books, 1989), pp. 30-31.

10 "Judges Must Speak Out for Peace," in Laffin and Montgomery, *op. cit.*, pp. 199-206.

11 Kownacki, Mary Lou, "Letter to an Experimenter with Truth" in *Sojourners*, May, 1983, p. 27.

Imprisoned for Sacramental Peacemaking

1 Feuerherd, Peter. "Why Would Anybody Want to Get Arrested?" *Salt*, Sept., 1988, p. 9.

2 Douglass, James, *The Nonviolent Cross* (New York: Macmillan, 1968), p. 44.

3 *Ibid.*, pp. 180-181.

4 Laffin, Arthur and Montgomery, Anne, *Swords into Plowshares* (San Francisco: Harper and Row, 1986), p. 93.

5 Douglass, James. "Loving Disobedience" in *Ground Zero*, 1986.

6 Laffin, *op. cit.*, p. 73-75.

7 Berrigan, Philip and McAlister, Elizabeth, *The Time's Discipline* (Baltimore: Fortkamp Pub. Co., 1988), p. 196.

8 McAlister, Elizabeth, "A Garden in Cracked Soil" in *Sojourners*, April, 1987, p. 16.

9 Frankel-Streit, Bill, *Letter to the Author*, February 6, 1991.

10 Dietrich, Jeff, *Reluctant Resister* (Greensboro, NC: Unicorn Press, 1983), p. 91.

11 Stringfellow, William, *A Second Birthday* (New York: Doubleday and Co., 1970), p. 133.

12 Fischer, Louis, *The Essential Gandhi* (New York: Vintage Books, 1962), p. 296.

13 Douglass, James, *Resistance and Contemplation* (New York: Doubleday, 1972), p. 172.

14 Fischer, *The Life of Mahatma Gandhi, op. cit.*, p. 79.

15 Green, Martin (Ed.), *Gandhi in India* (Boston: Univ. Press of New England, 1987), pp.39-40.

16 Fischer, *The Life of Mahatma Gandhi, op. cit.*, p. 272.

17 Fischer, *The Essential Gandhi, op. cit.*, p. 116.

18 *Ibid.*, pp. 176-177.

19 *Ibid.*, p. 275.

20 Gandhi, Mohandas, *Nonviolent Resistance* (New York: Schocken Books, 1951), pp. 65- 66.

21 *Ibid.*, p. 61.

22 *Ibid.*, p. 63.

23 Thoreau, Henry David, "On the Duty of Civil Disobedience," in *Walden and Civil Disobedience* (New York: New American Library, 1960), p. 233; Fischer, *The Life of Mahatma Gandhi, op. cit.*, p. 87.

24 Zahn, Gordan, *In Solitary Witness* (Collegeville, MN: The Liturgical Press, 1964), p.65.

25 King, Martin Luther, "The Great March to Freedom," Taped, June 23, 1964, in Detroit (Detroit: Motown Records, 1963).

26 Washington, James, *A Testament of Hope: The Essential Writings of Martin Luther King, Jr.* (San Francisco: Harper and Row, 1986), p. 290.

27 Miller, William Robert, *Nonviolence* (New York: Schocken Books, 1972), p. 154.

28 Ellsberg, Robert (Ed.), *By Little and By Little: The Selected Writings of Dorothy Day* (New York: Knopf Pub., 1983), p. 352.

29 *Ibid.*, p. 285.

30 Berrigan, Philip,*Widen the Prison Gates* (New York: Touchstone Books, 1973), p. 76.

31 Douglass, James, *op. cit.*, p. 44.

32 Berrigan, *op. cit.*, p. 48.

33 Berrigan, Philip. "Imprisonment Could Hardly Be More to the Point" in *National Catholic Reporter*, February 11, 1994, p. 17.

34 Berrigan, Daniel, *Lights On in the House of the Dead* (New York: Doubleday and Co.,1973), p. 131.

35 *Ibid.*, pp. 5-6.

REFERENCES

████████████████████

from Informed Consent... master reforms ..., 1994 p 8.

Berman, Daniel. Labor on the House... (New York:
Monthly Review Press, 1978.

About the Author

Rev. John Dear is an internationally recognized voice and leader for peace and nonviolence. A priest, activist and author, he served for years as the director of the Fellowship of Reconciliation, the largest interfaith peace organization in the US.

John has traveled the war zones of the world, been arrested some 85 times for peace, led Nobel Peace prize winners to Iraq, and given thousands of lectures on peace and justice across the US. He is a co-founder of Campaign Nonviolence and the Nonviolent Cities Project and founder and director of The Beatitudes Center for the Nonviolent Jesus (www.beatitudescenter.org)

His thirty five books include: *The Beatitudes of Peace*; *They Will Inherit the Earth*; *The Nonviolent Life*; *Radical Prayers*; *Walking the Way*; *A Persistent Peace*; *Jesus the Rebel*; *Peace Behind Bars;* and most recently, *Praise Be Peace: The Psalms of Peace and Nonviolence in a time of War and Climate Change*. He has been nominated many times for the Nobel Peace Prize, including by Archbishop Desmond Tutu.

www.johndear.org